COLONIAL AMERICA

VOLUME 3

DISEASE—GAMES AND SPORTS

CONSULTANT EDITOR: DR. D. THORP

Published 1998 by
Grolier Educational, Sherman Turnpike, Danbury, Connecticut 06816

© 1998 Brown Partworks Ltd

Set ISBN: 0-7172-9193-6
Volume ISBN: 0-7172-9196-0

Library of Congress Cataloging-in-Publication Data
Colonial America.
p.cm.—Includes bibliographical references and index.
Contents: v. 1. A-By—v. 2.C-De—v. 3. Di-Ga—v. 4. Ge-In—
v. 5. In-Marq—v. 6. Marr-Na—v. 7. Ne-Pe—v. 8. Ph-Re—
v. 9. Rh-St—v. 10. St-Z.

1. United States—History—Colonial period, ca. 1600–1775—
Encyclopedias. Juvenile. 2. United States—History—Revolution,
1775–1783—Encyclopedias. Juvenile. I. Grolier Educational (Firm)
II. Title: Colonial America
E188.C696   1998
973.2—DC21   97-44595
                                                             CIP
                                                             AC

For information address the publisher:
Grolier Educational, Sherman Turnpike, Danbury, Connecticut 06816

FOR BROWN PARTWORKS LTD
Editor: Clint Twist
Designer: Bradley Davis
Picture research: Sharon Southren
Text editor: Mike Sharpe

Printed in Singapore

CONTENTS

DISEASE

Columbus's voyage to North America began not only an exchange of cultures between the New and the Old World, but also an exchange of diseases that had equally dramatic and profound results. For the first time diseases from America, Europe, and Africa came together and forever changed the world.

People everywhere shared many sicknesses and ailments—the common cold for example—and everyone was susceptible to infections from burns or wounds, regardless of where they lived. Difficult pregnancies and childbirth often caused complications that led to the death of the mother. However, isolated by large bodies of water and separated by diet, climate, and habits, peoples on each side of the Atlantic had a number of diseases unique to their communities.

UNWELCOME VISITORS
When people of different continents met in North America, Native Americans were far more susceptible to new diseases than Europeans. Sealed off from the rest of the world, Native Americans were quite free of European diseases such as smallpox, measles, typhus, and dysentery. Unfortunately, they also had no immunity to those diseases.

Because of this lack of natural protection, when the Spanish began to conquer the Caribbean and Mexico, the native peoples were defeated as much by the diseases brought across the Atlantic by the Spanish as by Spanish guns. Epidemics of smallpox and dysentery destroyed 90 percent of the Native Americans in the area. Within 50 years of Columbus's arrival on the island of Hispaniola, the entire

native Taino population had died, either from being killed in fighting or from disease.

DISEASES SPREAD NORTH
It is believed that the bubonic plague, which had killed millions in Europe in the 14th century, was brought by the Spanish to Florida. By around 1613 it was found in all the colonies as far north as New England; white settlers suffered from smallpox too but had built up a certain resistance to it in

▲ Columbus lands in the New World. His contact with the locals began an exchange of diseases that had devastating results for the native population.

164

In hot weather the swampy bayous of Louisiana are perfect breeding grounds for disease. Native Americans habitually left such areas every summer and moved to cooler climates.

Europe. Within one generation, however, the colonists became almost as susceptible as the natives. The first recorded smallpox epidemic in North America occurred in 1667 on the eastern shore of Virginia. One-third of Virginia's Native Americans had fallen victim to the disease within 60 years.

The Europeans did not completely escape the exchange. Syphilis, a sexually transmitted disease that eventually spread throughout Europe, may well have been transmitted by the Native Americans. The slave ships bringing Africans to the colonial plantations also carried a deadly new strain of malaria, brought from West Africa, which caused an epidemic among whites and Native Americans in the mid-17th century. They also brought amoebic dysentery, which affected whites and natives alike.

DISEASES OF SLAVERY
West Africans seemed to have a natural defense against malaria. They had no immunity, however, to diseases such as measles, influenza,

pneumonia, and tuberculosis. Mortality rates among Africans in America were as high as 50 percent in the early 17th century. Weakened by the atrocious conditions on slave ships, enslaved Africans easily succumbed to malnutrition and disease. They were especially susceptible to lung and bronchial infections. After 1700, however, the numbers of slave deaths began to fall as many Africans came to North America by way of the Caribbean. The time they spent here allowed them to get used to a new environment.

AVOIDING DISEASE
People in the 17th and 18th centuries had little scientific knowledge of the causes of disease, and medicine was still very much in its infancy. All cultures had only a vague idea about how to stay healthy and as

▼ *Smallpox rarely strikes the same person twice. This poster claims that all the slaves on sale are free of smallpox and, even better, half of them have already suffered from the disease so will be immune.*

TO BE SOLD on board the Ship *Bance-Island,* on tuesday the 6th of *May* next, at *Ashley-Ferry*; a choice cargo of about 250 fine healthy NEGROES, just arrived from the Windward & Rice Coast. —The utmost care has already been taken, and shall be continued, to keep them free from the least danger of being infected with the SMALL-POX, no boat having been on board, and all other communication with people from *Charles-Town* prevented.
Austin, Laurens, & *Appleby.*
N. B. Full one Half of the above Negroes have had the SMALL-POX in their own Country.

a result, they treated disease with folkways rather than science.

The lifestyle of Native Americans helped them avoid situations that would make them ill. Living in small, isolated communities, for instance, prevented diseases from turning into epidemics. In addition, many tribes were nomadic, moving across the land according to the season and climate. Virginia's woodland tribes would break into smaller groups and move away from the swampy tidal rivers during the hot summer months.

MAGICAL MEDICINE

Native Americans believed that illness was caused by some bad spirit that upset the body's balance. If people could not remove the spirit alone, they turned to the tribal medicine man who used a combination of magic and natural medicines to cleanse the body. Sweat lodges, like saunas, were used to prevent and cure sickness.

Successive generations of Africans handed down tribal customs that they had brought from their homelands.

▶ *Smallpox was a highly contagious disease that left the sufferer covered in unsightly sores. It was responsible for the deaths of thousands of Native Americans after the arrival of European settlers.*

▼ *A carving of a Native American shaman, or medicine man, in the middle of a trance. His two helping spirits are given the appearance of animals.*

Many were similar to those used by Native Americans. Africans too believed that spirits controlled health and healing. Suffering could be caused by misbehavior, so it was up to the individual or the tribe to make things right through prayer and sacrifice. West-African tribes had medicine men, too, who used healing rituals, magic, and natural remedies.

Europeans had no better knowledge of the causes of infectious disease than their African or Native-American counterparts. While they did not directly believe in spirits, they did believe in the intervention of God in causing and curing illness. Like the Africans and natives, they concocted home-made remedies from plants and animals. Such cures were often all that was available in the fight against disease in the New World.

SEE ALSO
ENVIRONMENT ■ MEDICINE ■ RELIGION, NATIVE AMERICAN ■ SLAVE CULTURE ■ SLAVERY

DOMINION OF NEW ENGLAND

In 1686 the New England colonies were combined into a viceroyalty, governed by a representative of the English king and known as the Dominion of New England. The English government had wanted to merge the American colonies into a few large provinces for a long time, and James II was eager to see the formation of a single administration to bring the colonies under greater royal control. He had been alarmed at the contempt settlers had shown for the Navigation Acts, which restricted foreign trade with the colonies. James also wanted to tighten defense, fearing the growing power of France and believing it was trying to sabotage the important alliance between the English and the Iroquois tribes.

THE ARRIVAL OF ANDROS

The opportunity for this reorganization occurred after the old charter government of Massachusetts Bay was removed. The Dominion was founded, in temporary form, in June 1686 under the presidency of New Englander Joseph Dudley. It was formally established in December of the same year by the arrival of a new governor, Sir Edmund Andros. Massachusetts and New Hampshire were the first members. Rhode Island and Conecticut soon followed, and in 1688 New York, East Jersey, and West Jersey were added to the Dominion. This created a unit that proved too large for one governor to administer effectively.

Andros's strict, military-style administration created a great deal of hostility. The Puritan population was also antagonized by the establishment of the Congregational Church in the Dominion. In the spring of 1689 news of King James's expulsion from England reached the colonies. Most of the colonists declared their allegiance to the new king, William. Andros was arrested by the Boston militia: his army had not been paid for months and put up no opposition.

The failure of the Dominion was a clear warning to England that the colonies could only be governed by smaller local assemblies free from direct control.

Governor Andros proclaims the Dominion of New England. Andros had served James II in New York for 10 years; his friendship and loyalty to the king and his military background convinced the colonists that James was trying to turn America into a military garrison.

SEE ALSO

GLORIOUS REVOLUTION ■ MASSACHUSETTS
■ NAVIGATION ACTS ■ NEW ENGLAND

SIR FRANCIS DRAKE

Sir Francis Drake was born in Tavistock, England, around 1541. His father was a tenant farmer and lay preacher, but Drake chose a career at sea. In his early twenties he began work for Sir John Hawkins, whose family had established trading connections with the New World. Drake's daring adventures during an expedition to South America in 1567 came to the attention of the English queen, Elizabeth I, and she commissioned Drake to make attacks on Spanish ships transporting gold from the Caribbean to Spain.

For two years Drake attacked Spanish settlements and gold fleets. After returning to England in 1573 with a fortune in gold and jewels, he was put in charge of a naval force sent to crush a rebellion in Ireland.

SAILING THE SOUTHERN OCEANS

In the mid-1570s rumors began to circulate of a great continent in the southern oceans, which mapmakers had named Terra Australis. With the financial backing of the queen Drake left Plymouth on December 13, 1577, with a fleet of five ships. Led by Drake's flagship, the *Pelican*, later renamed the *Golden Hind*, three of the ships tried to sail through the Strait of Magellan, at the southernmost tip of South America, in August of 1578. Drake continued up the west coast of South America, raiding Spanish settlements and looting ships as he went.

Laden down with treasure, Drake followed the coast north as far as Vancouver Bay, searching for a route

▶ *The* Golden Hind *was the only ship of Drake's fleet to pass through the Strait of Magellan.*

▲ *Francis Drake was the first Englishman to sail across the Pacific Ocean.*

that would lead him back to the Atlantic. The severe weather forced him to turn back, and the fleet moored for seven weeks at Drake's Bay, north of San Francisco. Claiming the surrounding land—which he named New Albion— for Queen Elizabeth, Drake explored the California coast. He then sailed westward. In the Philippines Drake carried out attacks on Spanish treasure ships before leaving the Moluccan Islands (part of Indonesia) to return to England. On September 26, 1580, he arrived in Plymouth after the second round-the-world voyage in history.

Drake returned to the Americas several times with raiding parties. In 1585 he plundered the Spanish settlement at St. Augustine in Florida. The following year, with Sir Walter Raleigh, he ferried many of the Roanoke colonists home to England. Drake undertook his final expedition in 1595 but contracted dysentery and died on January 28, 1596.

SEE ALSO
RALEIGH, SIR WALTER ■ ROANOKE
■ ST. AUGUSTINE ■ SAN FRANCISCO

JONATHAN EDWARDS

E

Jonathan Edwards (1703–1758) was a leading figure in the Great Awakening, the dramatic revival of an emotional, passionate way of preaching and worshipping that swept through the English colonies. One of the foremost American religious scholars, Edwards was the son of a Connecticut pastor, the only boy in a family of 11 children. At the age of 13 he entered Yale College. He showed great promise, graduating at the top of his class at the age of just 17, then spending two years studying divinity.

Edwards became pastor of the Congregationalist church at Northampton, Massachusetts, in 1727 and in the same year was married to Sarah Pierrepont, with whom he was to raise 11 children.

He felt that the people in his neighborhood lacked faith in God and preached sermons to "frighten people away from hell." The sermons successfully converted many, and by 1735 he could say that "the town seemed to be full of the presence of God." Contemporary preachers such as the dramatic young English sermonizer, George Whitefield, were having a similar effect. Whitefield was partly responsible for the Great Awakening in the church during the mid-1700s. Edwards was impressed by Whitefield and preached his own form of "revivalism." He published many sermons; perhaps the best-known is one delivered at Enfield, Massachusetts, in 1741, *Sinners in the Hands of an Angry God*. He also wrote numerous religious works looking at Christian beliefs in terms of the philosophy of the time.

After a dispute concerning religious principles, Edwards left Northampton

in 1750 to become pastor of a Native-American community at Stockbridge. He continued to write treatises on religious philosophy, on the glory of God, and on how faith in God was more important than a person's behavior. He quit preaching to take up a post as president of the College of New Jersey (later Princeton) just two months before his death from smallpox in March 1758.

SEE ALSO

CONNECTICUT ■ GREAT AWAKENING
■ MASSACHUSETTS ■ RELIGION, ANGLICAN
■ WHITEFIELD, GEORGE

▲ *Edwards had a great many interests and wrote manuscripts on subjects such as botany and optics—the study of light. Throughout his life he recorded his thoughts in numerous hand-sewn notebooks.*

E ENVIRONMENT

The first Europeans to explore the American continent found a land characterized by dramatic contrasts and extremes, with rain forests, deserts, plains, and arctic areas. At the beginning of the 16th century there were only 1–2 million Native Americans within the present-day borders of the United States. The size of their population and their limited exploitation of the land meant that the habitat was largely wild.

A HOSTILE RECEPTION

European settlers came across many obstacles that were unfamiliar to them but the blizzards, dust storms, ferocious animals, locusts, and (occasionally) unfriendly humans failed to dim their appreciation of the vast, fertile land with its plentiful natural resources.

Colonization by Europeans resulted in a transformation of this largely untouched land. The attitudes, demands, and size of the new colonial population dramatically reshaped the environments they inhabited.

One of the reasons for this change was the entirely different attitudes of the native and the European toward nature. The Native American's relationship with the land was based on the belief that plants and animals were gifts of nature to satisfy human needs, but that humans also had a responsibility to use these gifts with care and restraint. They believed that the natural and the spiritual worlds were closely related, seeing animals as their ancestors.

The European settlers, by contrast, sought to master the environment and saw it as an economic resource. The natives' view of their habitat as a tribal home, with communities able to freely cross land during seasonal migrations, was replaced by European ideas of

▶ *Catching fish through holes in the ice. Natives were careful not to overfish the rivers and did not fish during the spawning season.*

◀ *The settlers brought with them a totally new form of land management. The land on this 18th-century farm has been stripped of trees and divided into fenced-off fields.*

private property. Maps were produced, and land ownership was decided by deed. Areas of land were divided up, fenced off, and either auctioned or rented out by companies to any individual with money.

At first European habitation was shaped according to the coastal communication links with Europe. As time passed, settlers advanced up rivers, still maintaining contact with the sea, and began permanent settlements by building homes. The natural landscapes changed as towns such as Boston expanded: it grew from a population of 7,000 in 1690 to 17,000 by 1740. Even small communities such as Essex, Connecticut, which had grown from only three original settlers, could have an effect on the landscape. The colonists built a wharf in 1664 and altered the flow of the Falls River by building a dam in 1689.

In contrast, the number of native settlements dwindled, partly because

of European diseases. Smallpox had killed almost half of the Cherokee population by 1730 and a similar proportion of Catawbas by 1759.

Most native tribes in North America lived by agriculture but the European agricultural techniques used by the

The deserts of Arizona were occupied only by Native Americans who knew how to survive in such an arid climate.

E

BOSTON'S FIRST TOWN-HOUSE
1657-1711

colonists forced a change on the natural environment. Although the first European fishermen and traders did not farm, their successors plowed the fertile land along the coast and were soon producing food for themselves. Farms began to spring up everywhere in the wake of westward expansion, and much woodland was cleared for farming and pasture. Settlers also began trading and exporting large quantities of hard- and softwoods. Many trees were felled to provide valuable lumber, tar, and resin for a growing local and overseas market.

Captain John Smith, one of the leading figures in the community at Jamestown, Virginia, reported that by 1609 almost all the woodland around Jamestown had been cleared. In 1626, just six years after the Plymouth Colony was founded, tree-cutting there had to be regulated.

The efficiency of the metal-headed ax that was used to fell trees, the girdling system used to kill trees, and the practice of clearing woodland by fire to produce valuable wood-ash fertilizer cleared forests at great speed. Crops were then planted and animals raised on soil that had been enriched by the ash.

▲ *Boston was a busy town even at the beginning of the 18th century. The rapid growth of such towns led to a great demand for timber to build the wooden houses and fences.*

▶ *The busy levee (wharf) at New Orleans. The town's position on the great Mississippi River was perfect for a port, but the local environment did present problems. The low-lying land and high rainfall of the area meant that it was always liable to flooding.*

Carried out so quickly and extensively, this process was very harmful to the land since it eventually caused the soil to lose its nutrients. The productivity of the soil declined over about five years. Agricultural land that had once been rich became barren. The land had no trees to protect it from the elements and no dead leaves to add nutrients to the soil when they decayed. Such soils also encouraged harmful toxins and parasites to develop, especially when only one type of crop was planted.

There was so much land available that, instead of trying to restore the land's fertility, farmers simply moved to uncleared areas and started again, leaving a path of waste land behind them. Abandoned land did eventually recover, however, and after a time natural plantlife would reappear.

NEW GROWTH

A large number of new plants were introduced to America by the colonists. One of the first new species to appear was the peach, first cultivated by the Spanish and French in the 16th century. When the English

explored the interior of Georgia and Carolina, they found peach trees flourishing in native orchards. As the natives traveled north, the peach tree followed, but as their communities declined and their gardens were abandoned, the peach grew wild.

New crops such as wheat were brought over as seeds by the settlers. But Old World weeds also traveled with these seeds and reproduced rapidly in disturbed soils. Some weeds, such as white clover and Kentucky bluegrass, were planted as food for livestock and soon spread to all 13 colonies. English settlers crossing the Appalachians to reach Kentucky were surprised to find that European weeds had arrived before them. Other weeds, such as the nettle,

▲ *Trees shelter the land and protect it from wind and rain erosion. Their dead leaves also add nutrients. If forest clearance is not controlled, the land may become barren.*

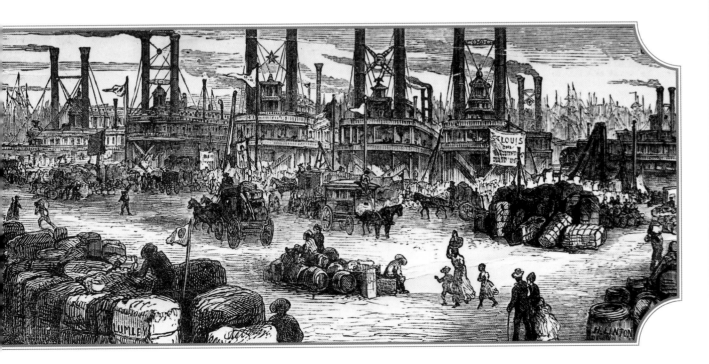

▶ *Much of the awe-inspiring landscape of America was out of reach of the colonists and remained unaffected by settlement. This dramatic painting is of the Yellowstone canyon.*

arrived by accident and flourished wherever there was cool, moist land. The Englishman John Josselyn visited New England in 1638 and 1663 and counted at least 22 familiar weeds that had crossed the Atlantic. Native weeds, such as Manitoba and Dakota grasses, were often replaced by more aggressive Old World weeds or else cleared by European farmers. Many of the grasses that grew east of the Mississippi lacked the qualities needed to resist European farm animals, which ate them down to the roots.

Despite these changes, many native species continued to flourish. In the central regions of America the environment proved to be too hostile for the introduced plants, and native weeds like the buffalo and grama grasses continued to survive on the Great Plains. Natives also taught the settlers about the values of many wild plants, which they learned to cultivate.

THE EFFECT ON WILDLIFE

The animal life of the land also felt the effects of colonization. Like the natives, Europeans also killed animals

for food, especially when their crops were poor, but the desire for other animal products—particularly skins and fur—caused widescale and uncontrolled hunting. The fur trade expanded with assistance from the native tribes and the spread of

▶ *Different environments have their own ecosystems, in which all living things depend on each other for survival. The red fox was affected by the hunting of beavers, which destroyed its food source. The fox managed to survive, however, and is now widespread over most of the U.S.*

wild dogs such as coyotes, and cats such as bobcats.

Even the ocean could not escape the influence of the settlers. The waters between Cape Cod and Cape Race in Newfoundland were ideal fishing grounds. The cod, herring, mackerel, and bass caught here were in such great demand in local and export markets that the area was in danger of being overfished.

The balance of the environment was also affected by the range of domestic animals that the colonists introduced from Europe. Even honeybees were brought to Virginia in the early 1620s to pollinate crops. Inevitably, some domestic animals became wild (known as feral), since it was common practice to allow livestock to graze freely. The razorback—a breed of pig that had been introduced from Europe— roamed fields and forests and became a serious problem in North America.

Europeans also introduced vermin from the Old World. By the time the explorer Samuel de Champlain was making his voyages to the New World, black rats, which had swum ashore from English ships, were commonly sighted in settlements. In 1609 they almost destroyed Jamestown. The Virginia colony was only two years old when thousands of rats consumed its food stores. By the mid-18th century the deadly disease rabies had been brought to the colonies by rats.

In just two centuries the impact of European settlers on the environment was more dramatic than that of the Native-American tribes that had populated North America for thousands of years.

SEE ALSO
COUREURS DE BOIS ▥ DISEASE ▥ FARMING
▥ FISHING ▥ FORESTRY ▥ FOOD AND DRINK
▥ FUR TRADE ▥ HUNTING ▥ RICE ▥ TOBACCO

▼ By the beginning of the 17th century, rats had arrived in North America. They were transported there in the holds of ships.

firearms. The environmental effects of hunting were far reaching. As the beaver population decreased—the beaver was favored by European hatmakers for its soft fur—the wildlife that lived in the beavers' dams and ponds, such as black ducks and muskrats, became threatened. Many native animals were also hunted or trapped because they were unwelcome on the colonists' land. Livestock was preyed on by bears,

OLAUDAH EQUIANO

Among the hundreds of thousands of Africans captured for the slave trade with North America in the 18th century was a little boy from the Benin region of West Africa. He and his sister were playing while their parents were out working in the fields when the slavers grabbed them and shipped them off to the West Indies to be sold. The boy's name was Olaudah Equiano, and he was born around 1745—he was not sure of the exact date. He was about 11 years old when he was forced to endure a long journey across the Atlantic in the hold of a slave ship.

LEARNING ON BOARD

Equiano was fortunate to survive the crossing and was sold to a British slave-ship captain, Michael Pascal. On board Pascal's ship he learned the trades of ironsmith, cook, steward, and barber, and was taught to speak English and to read the Bible. During his time as a slave he sailed between the Caribbean and mainland colonies and became one of the few black sea captains, known as "Black Jacks."

Equiano was sold by Pascal to another master in 1763. By 1766 Equiano had saved enough money to buy his freedom. He changed his slave name, Gustavus Vassa, back to his original name as soon as he was at liberty to do so. As an experienced seaman Equiano was chosen to organize a scheme for returning freed slaves to Sierra Leone in West Africa. The conditions on board these ships were as bad as the slave ships, and he gave up the job in protest.

Equiano then went to England, where he became involved in the anti-slavery movement. His accounts of the conditions of slavery were powerful propaganda for the campaign.

English relatives of Captain Pascal took him under their wing while he was in England and helped him continue his education. In 1789 he published an autobiography, *The Interesting Narrative of Olaudah Equiano, or Gustavus Vassa, the*

▲ *A portrait of Equiano Olaudah painted when he was in England. Despite his poor beginnings, Equiano became a member of London society.*

African. It was an instant best-seller and an important contribution to the antislavery campaign.

Exactly how true it all was has never really been agreed, but it was a colorful and simply written book that captured the imagination of people all over the world. It was also one of the first published autobiographies of a slave. Equiano stayed in England and married an Englishwoman, Susanna Cullen, in 1792. Although they are believed to have had two daughters, nothing is known about his family—his autobiography is his only memorial. He died in London in 1797.

SEE ALSO

FREE BLACKS ▪ SLAVE TRADE ▪ SLAVERY

▼ *Equiano's West African home of Benin, shown in this 18th-century map, was the scene of much slave trading.*

EYEWITNESS

FROM THE AUTOBIOGRAPHY OF OLAUDAH EQUIANO.

❝ *The stench of the hold while we were on the coast was so intolerably loathsome, that it was dangerous to remain there for any time, and some of us had been permitted to stay on the deck for the fresh air; but now that the whole ship's cargo were confined together, it became absolutely pestilential. The closeness of the place, and the heat of the climate, added to the number in the ship, which was so crowded that each had scarcely room to turn himself, almost suffocated us. This produced copious perspirations, so that the air soon became unfit for respiration, from a variety of loathsome smells, and brought on a sickness among the slaves, of which many died—thus falling victims to the improvident avarice, as I may call it, of their purchasers.* ❞

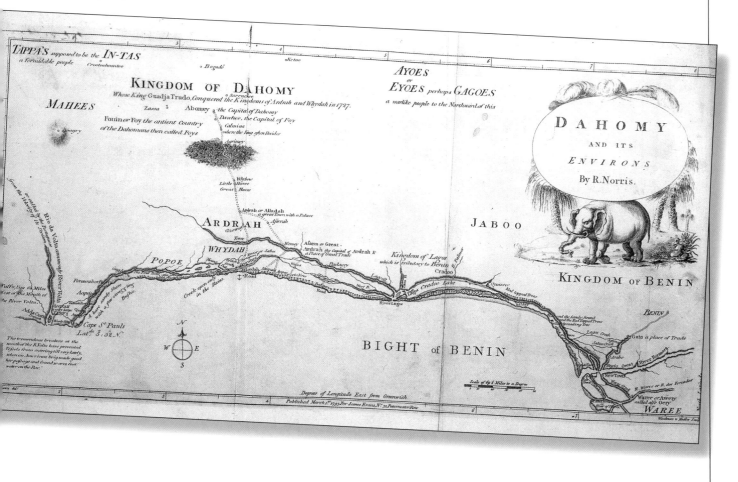

FAMILY LIFE

◀ *Many of the families who ventured beyond the frontier were quite isolated and communities took a long time to develop.*

▼ *Work around the home and farm was strictly divided between the husband and wife. Women were responsible for domestic chores and preparing the food.*

A merican colonists tried in many ways to re-create the culture of their homelands in their new environment. They built houses, worshipped God, made laws, and structured their families in the ways that were familiar to them. But the new and different conditions the settlers found in America meant that many aspects of their lives had to change. Family life in particular was affected by the circumstances and hardships of the New World. By the end of the colonial period the traditional family structure that had been so familiar in Europe gave way to a uniquely American style of family life.

The ideal family in Europe consisted of a father and a mother, their children, and—if they were

wealthy—servants and various apprentices. Each family was headed by a father who was responsible for the welfare and good behavior of his household (this is called a patriarchal system). Everyone in the household owed him total obedience in return. A well-ordered family benefited both the community and the nation as a whole. The family had almost become a public institution.

A SURPLUS OF MEN

Although colonists tried to re-create this model in America, colonial families eventually became far less ordered than those in the Old World. Family life in the Chesapeake Bay colonies and the South took longer to develop than in the other colonies. The large numbers of young, single men and small numbers of women meant there was an unbalanced population. This, together with high death rates and periods of native hostilities, stopped families becoming firmly established for nearly a century.

In all areas it was practical for parents to make their sons independent as soon as possible. The availability of land on the frontier made this especially easy. As a result, the very early frontier settlements

consisted mostly of single-person male households. The shortage of women limited the number of families. The absence of families delayed the development of institutions such as churches and schools.

The instability in family life in the Chesapeake Bay area meant that life was less strictly controlled. Young men no longer sought permission to marry, and marriages were not arranged by parents. Daughters often inherited their fathers' lands, wives controlled their husbands' estates, and women were more able to "marry up," that is, to marry a man in a higher social class. These practices were all rare in Europe at the time.

MARRYING AND REMARRYING

In the Chesapeake Bay area, on average, women married at 25 and men at 27; younger than in England. Only one marriage in three, however, lasted longer than 10 years. Because death rates were so high, losing a partner was a common occurrence. Most of the adults who died also left behind children. In the early Chesapeake Bay society, half of all children could expect to lose at least one parent by the age of nine; three-quarters would have lost their parents

▲ *The family unit was very important to the Puritans, and its stability was largely responsible for their successful communities. This family is attending a bible reading together.*

F by the time they were 21. Since a colonial family functioned best with both a mother and a father, remarriage was a common experience in the Chesapeake colonies. As a result, most families became combinations of step-children and step-parents, half-brothers and sisters, widowed aunts, orphaned nieces, nephews, and so on. Family life became complex and unpredictable.

EQUAL NUMBERS

The Puritan colonies of New England were far more traditional and, as a result, very stable. Of the Puritan immigrants, 70 percent came as part of a family. This, combined with lower death rates, kept the ratio of men to women more balanced. Women married at an older age than women in the Chesapeake area. Strong patriarchal families that promoted a community spirit were quickly and firmly established. Institutions such as the church and powerful community leaders and clergymen also had a steadying effect on family life.

▲ *In the early 17th century family life was very structured. This portrait shows just how formal it could be.*

▼ *A portrait from the end of the 18th century suggests that family life was more relaxed.*

Because they generally married at an older age, young men and women stayed in the family home for much longer. They helped tend the farm, obeying the authority of the head of the household.

It was economic changes in New England that eventually changed the character of the family. Land became scarce as the population grew. Young men began to leave their families to look for work in the new towns. By the early years of the 18th century family ties had slowly loosened and changed, just as they had earlier in the Chesapeake Bay area. The marriage age fell; daughters married out of birth order; romantic love played a role in choosing a partner.

THE MODERN FAMILY IS BORN

The roots of today's modern family can be seen in the middle colonies, where settlers came from a variety of backgrounds. There the nuclear family (a father, mother, and their children) lived in an independent household with other generations living nearby. Parents had little authority over grown-up children, and sons became independent early in life. On average, women had fewer children. By the 18th century the freedom of individuals was more important than their role within the community.

F

Family life still had common threads. Most colonial families earned their living from agriculture, which depended on the husband, wife, children, and servants all working together. Men and women had different roles within the family. Men tended animals, cultivated fields, and provided wood for the fire. Women were responsible for domestic work: grinding corn, making bread, churning butter, sewing, washing, and mending. All occupied their own place within the family, but they all contributed to the family's well-being.

Both men and women had a life in the community outside the family. White men who owned property could vote, serve on a jury, hold public office, and join the militia. Women were prevented by law from doing these things, but they still had a role to play. Women kept close to home, and family and neighbors made up their world. They helped other women with childbirth, they tended the sick, and they cared for the poor.

Among the early European colonists lived two other groups of people—Native Americans and slaves

from West Africa. Each had their own traditions of family life. For both of these peoples, the individual and their close family worked for the survival and success of the community, the tribe, or the village. In many native and West African societies families depended on the work of the women, who farmed the land and produced all domestic goods. Men contributed by hunting and fishing and defending the community. Native Americans and Africans often had a "matrilineal" society—position and property were inherited through the mother.

CARING SOCIETIES

Slave families, of course, suffered the greatest damage to family life. Ripped from their homeland and culture, they struggled to establish some form of family life in America. Marriages and families were generally encouraged by white owners although slave families were not recognized in law. Families were frequently split up when slaves were bought and sold. As a result, African-American slaves developed "kinship networks" that consisted of a large group of people who were probably not related but who acted as a family, taking care of one another.

The unique circumstances and environment of the New World slowly, subtly, and dramatically changed the traditional structure and role of the family. Families gradually became more independent of the community they lived in, and they were not as closely involved in its organization. By the end of the colonial era family structure mirrored the new American society that was emerging—a republican society based on the freedom of the individual.

▼ *A household in Kentucky. The home life of a wealthy land owner included a large network of family, servants, and slaves.*

SEE ALSO

CHILDREN ■ FRONTIER ■ MARRIAGE ■ WOMEN'S ROLES

FARMING

From the time the first settlements were established until the Revolutionary War, most colonists earned their living from the land. Nine out of 10 Americans were farmers, and most white farmers owned the land on which they worked.

Although agriculture represented a chance for independence and wealth, early attempts at farming by the settlers were not always successful. Many had not farmed in the Old World and so did not have the necessary skills, but even those who came with agricultural knowledge had to adjust their methods to suit North America's different soils and climates. Each of the colonies developed differently, but all borrowed and learned from the Native Americans, who had spent centuries developing

an agricultural system well-suited to the local terrain. Native-American agriculture relied on simple tools such as wooden hoes and digging sticks, but the crops they planted and harvested became the mainstay of the newly arrived European farmers.

PLANTING IN THREES

Corn, beans, and squash, nicknamed "the three sisters," provided a balanced diet for both humans and livestock. For hundreds of years Indians had cleared openings in the forests and then planted the three different plants together in small hills or mounds of soil. As the corn grew up tall and straight, the stalks provided support for the bean and squash vines. When these crops had worn out the soil, the forest clearings

▲ *The Native Americans had long been farming the land when the settlers arrived and knew how to get the most from their fields. Growing food was traditionally the job of the women in the tribe, as it also was for the Africans who were brought to America as slaves.*

LESSONS IN FARMING

Because they were unfamiliar with agricultural practices in the New World, the first European settlers were often in danger of starving. The lives of many of the first Pilgrims to arrive from England were saved by a Native American named Squanto. He combined agricultural practices from the Old and New World to help the settlers produce a successful corn crop.

Squanto was a member of the Wampanoag tribe living in what is now Massachusetts. He had been captured by the Spanish and taken to Europe in the early 1600s. From there he made his way to England and then returned to his homeland in 1619 as a pilot for an English sea captain. Upon his return he found that his tribe had all died, so he befriended the settlers at Plymouth Colony.

He taught them how to fish and how to grow corn. It was Squanto who showed the Pilgrims how to put each corn plant in its own mound of earth, and place a fish in the mound so that it could fertilize the plant as it decayed. In doing so, Squanto was combining techniques from two worlds. Although the Indians grew corn in hills, they did not use fish as fertilizer. It is likely that Squanto learned this agricultural technique in Spain or England.

Pilgrims appreciated the fact that Squanto's advice had saved them. They called him "a spetiall instrument sent of God for their good beyond their expectation."

Squanto also used his knowledge of English to negotiate a treaty between the natives and settlers. He helped form a bridge between the two cultures that unfortunately ended when he died in 1622.

were abandoned so the soil could recover. New clearings were then opened up and the cycle repeated.

In addition to the three sisters a number of other New World crops were adopted by settlers from Europe and Africa, including white potatoes, sweet potatoes, peanuts, tomatoes, pumpkins, cotton, and tobacco. No crop was more valuable than corn. It was easy to grow, easy to harvest, easy to grind into cornmeal for bread, and easy to feed to farm animals.

Corn was grown everywhere in the American colonies, but it was more important in areas such as New England, where the poor, rocky soil and cool climate made it harder to grow other crops. Wheat, for instance, was grown in the Old World and used to make bread. When farmers tried to grow this grain in New England, however, it often failed because of a disease the settlers called "blast," later identified as black stem rust. As a consequence, these farmers turned

F more and more to corn. "Johnnycake," a type of cornbread, was found on every dinner table, and for a while corn was so important in the colonies that it was even used as money.

FARMING IN THE NORTH

The poor New England soils made it more profitable for many farmers to raise livestock than to grow crops for cash. Cattle and pigs provided meat that was packed into barrels and shipped from trading towns like Boston and New London to the West Indies. Sheep were raised for their wool, which was turned into fabric.

There were pockets of rich farmland in New England—the Connecticut River Valley, for example—where large amounts of tobacco were successfully grown. For the most part, however, New

▲ *This painting, entitled* The Residence of David Twining, *shows a prosperous, well-stocked farm as it looked in 1785. By the end of the 18th century agriculture in the colonies was becoming more organized and efficient.*

◀ *Corn was the most important crop grown in the colonies. The settlers quickly learned how to cultivate this new and versatile plant that was unknown in Europe.*

England's family farms were smaller than those in the rest of the country, and land was distributed and shared much more equally. For many years the villages had an area of common land where everybody's livestock could be grazed, and often the townspeople shared the cost of buying a bull for breeding purposes. Agriculture in New England could not meet the demands of the population, however, and it was the only region of the country that continued to import more food than it exported.

The population of the middle Atlantic colonies—New York, New Jersey, Pennsylvania, Delaware, and the western part of Virginia—were blessed with far more productive agricultural land and a milder climate than their northern neighbors. The area was dubbed the "Colonial Breadbasket" because of all the wheat that was grown here. Not only did wheat seem to resist the "blast" better here, but the richer land produced

F

more grain per acre. The farms were slightly larger than those in the north (100–200 acres), and villages and farms were scattered across the country instead of crowded together. Every farmer here grew a variety of crops, but wheat was best for making money. Excess grain was taken to cities such as Baltimore, where it was ground into flour and shipped to the other colonies and the West Indies.

Before the rise of wheat production in America flour for the West Indies had come from England. The middle colonies could get flour to the Caribbean in half the time (one month instead of two), and it tended not to spoil as quickly as the flour that came from England's cooler climate.

Another distinct type of agriculture developed in the southern settlements of Virginia, where reliance on a single crop created larger plantations. Tobacco was the staple crop of the Virginia economy for much of the colonial period. The plant, nicknamed "the esteemed weed," was grown and shipped to Europe in huge quantities and became so profitable for the colonists in the early 1600s that it was planted in every square inch of dirt, including the streets of Jamestown.

Tobacco growers soon found themselves locked into a vicious cycle by their success. Not only did tobacco require hard work by many people, but it removed all the nutrients from the soil, making it worthless for other crops. After growing tobacco in a field for three to four seasons, farmers had to let that plot of land lay fallow (unplanted) for up to 20 years before it was fertile again. As a consequence, planters had to keep clearing more land every couple of years.

Single-crop systems also developed in the Carolinas and Georgia, where rice and indigo, a plant that produced a violet-blue dye, were the moneymakers. Slaves knowledgeable in rice cultivation were brought in from West Africa specially to work these plantations under harsh and back-breaking conditions.

EXCHANGING KNOWLEDGE

Native-American farmers were also influential in the Spanish West—including areas of New Mexico, Texas, and California—where they were able to give Spanish settlers valuable help and advice in growing crops. Unlike the English colonies, where profit was top priority, the Spanish settlers were concerned only with growing enough crops to feed their families. In the 1690s they also established missions in these areas and converted many natives to Catholicism.

At the same time, they taught them new agricultural methods, which included raising livestock and using irrigation to water crops in the dry climate. In California there were a few successful attempts at raising grapes for winemaking in the 1770s. By far

▼ *A New England farm as it looked at the end of the 18th century.*

F the biggest success in the Spanish West, however, was cattle raising, an activity that continues to this day in much of the West.

Livestock imported from Europe—cattle, horses, pigs, sheep, and chickens—proved profitable in most areas of the North American colonies. The hilly pastures in the backcountry of Virginia and the Carolinas were too steep to plant crops but proved especially suited to grazing animals.

Cattle were driven to these meadows in the spring and left in the cool mountain fields during the summer, where they fattened on the lush grass. In the fall the animals were rounded up and driven to markets such as Philadelphia and Charleston. The colonial meat trade coming out of these two market cities provided food for other colonies and for the West Indies. In addition to meat the cow hides provided leather and tallow, or animal fat, which was made into soap and candles.

In contrast to the native tribes, where women were the ones who grew food and worked in the fields, it was the men of settler families who traditionally tended the land. The women looked after the home and only got involved by processing the food produced by their husbands. On farms everywhere, especially near Boston and Philadelphia, women milked cows and made butter. They then sold their product in the cities, bringing in cash for the family.

A SLOW AND DIFFICULT TASK

Although most people in colonial America made their living from the soil, their methods were often crude and even destructive. In the beginning plows were rare in the New World, but even after they became more commonplace, they were heavy, clumsy tools that were tiring for both the farmer and his animals to work. For the first hundred years the moldboard, the part of the plow that cuts into and turns over the soil, was made of wood. Soil stuck to the moldboard, and farmers frequently had to stop and clean the gummed-up

▼ *This back-country farm has been reconstructed in Kentucky. The rugged terrain of the frontier was more suited to raising animals such as cattle than growing crops.*

A collection of early English plows that were exported to colonial America. No matter what their size or shape, plows were difficult to use, and plowing a field demanded much time and effort from the farmer and his horses.

F

plow. At the beginning of the 18th century blacksmiths started to improve the wooden plow by taking a piece of metal and wrapping it around the wooden moldboard. This proved more effective because the smoother surface of the iron stopped the soil from sticking. However, it still took two men and two or three horses (or four to six oxen) a whole day to plow just one or two acres of land.

When the time came to sow seeds, the broadcast method was used. Handfuls of seed were simply tossed out onto the newly turned soil. Some plants came up close together and competed with each other for nutrients; others were too far apart. Either way, it was hard for the farmer to farm efficiently.

Harvest methods were equally slow. Corn was picked, husked, and shelled by hand. Even harder and more dangerous was the harvest of small grains such as wheat, rye, and oats. Workers had to bend over, grab a handful of stalks, and then slice them off using a half-moon-shaped blade called a sickle. Many a finger was sliced with a sharp sickle.

Many farmers in America did not practice wise agriculture. For the most part they cleared the land, planted crops until the soil's nutrients were used up, and then moved on to the next field. It was a system designed to make money for the farmer, not to conserve the land, although when labor was in short supply and land was plentiful, it was often the best way to farm.

German settlers, on the other hand, tended to stay put and worked on improving their farms for their children and grandchildren. They recognized the value in spreading manure to enrich the fields, for example, and their neat, tidy farms were known throughout the colonies.

The early settlers were quick to establish successful and profitable farms and plantations, but their approach to agriculture often took a heavy toll on the land in the long run.

SEE ALSO

▓ ENVIRONMENT ▓ FOOD AND DRINK ▓ IMMIGRATION, GERMAN ▓ INDIGO ▓ LIVESTOCK ▓ PLANTATIONS ▓ RICE ▓ TOBACCO ▓ TRADE ▓ WEST INDIES

FESTIVALS

A Native-American harvest festival in the late 16th century. Notice the dancers' wooden rattles and the carved faces on the posts.

Every group of people in colonial America set aside time to relax and enjoy special foods and games that were not part of the drudgery of everyday life. Some of these celebrations were seasonal, meaning they honored the coming of spring or a successful harvest. Some celebrations marked important Christian religious dates like Christmas and Easter, while others were held to commemorate official events such as Guy Fawkes Day or Election Day.

A number of Native-American festivals coincided with seasonal occurrences. The Maple Ceremony was held in the spring when the sap in sugar maple trees could be harvested to make a sweet syrup. There were also native celebrations to mark the planting and harvesting of crops like strawberries and green beans. Many of these special days were marked by a game that resembles modern-day lacrosse and could sometimes involve all the inhabitants of the village.

The Green Corn Feast was celebrated by the Iroquois at the beginning of corn harvest, whereas the Mid-Winter Ceremony was held at the start of the new year. During the

Mid-Winter Ceremony all of the hearth fires in the village were extinguished, even the sacred fire that burned in the council house. The entire village fasted, prayed, and bathed. When the rituals were complete, the sacred fire was rekindled, and the rest of the village fires were relit from it. The Native-American tribes had many different types of rituals, which were celebrated with dancing, feasting, and religious ceremonies.

EUROPEAN INFLUENCES

The type of festivals and celebrations brought by European settlers to the New World differed according to their region of origin and religious affiliation. In New England, where Puritanism was the dominant religion, celebrations were considered a sign of wastefulness and laziness. The Puritans believed in a church free of excess and looked upon those who celebrated any religious holiday as having Catholic leanings.

Christmas, Easter, and even May Day celebrations were banned by law in the 17th century. Governor William Bradford of the Plymouth Colony chastized the colonists for playing a ball game in the streets on Christmas Day in 1621. In England and parts of Europe May Day was celebrated to mark the arrival of spring and the renewed fertility of the soil. A tall, brightly painted pole (maypole) was put up in the center of the village, and people holding colored ribbons tied to the top danced around in circles. In 1628 residents in Sir Thomas Morton's Massachusetts settlement who erected a maypole angered the governor, who ordered the pole to be chopped down.

Unable to celebrate religious holidays, New Englanders turned to other means to break the monotony of daily life. They would flock to town to watch funerals and public executions. Election Day, when the local government officers were chosen, was sure to draw a crowd.

During the early days of colonial settlement all able-bodied men were required to train as soldiers in case they were needed to defend the frontier. These militia men would gather together to march and train, but also to compete in foot races and shooting matches on a day called Training Day in New England and Muster Day in the rest of the colonies. The atmosphere was much like that of

▼ *A German family celebrating St. Nicholas's Day in December. German colonists brought this festival with them when they settled in America, where St. Nicholas's Day became part of the Christmas celebrations.*

F

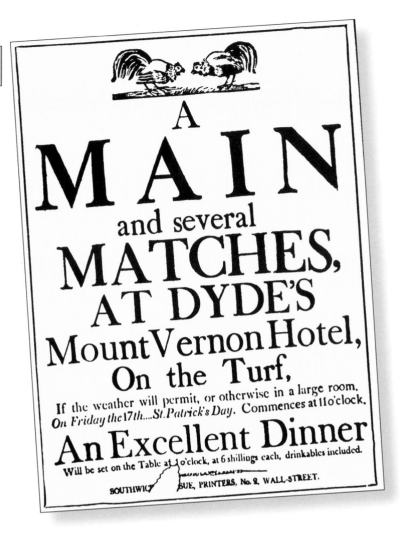

A MAIN
and several
MATCHES,
AT DYDE'S
Mount Vernon Hotel,
On the Turf,

If the weather will permit, or otherwise in a large room.
On Friday the 17th....St.Patrick's Day. Commences at 11o'clock.

An Excellent Dinner

Will be set on the Table at 1 o'clock, at 6 shillings each, drinkables included.

SOUTHWIC   SUE, PRINTERS, No. 2, WALL-STREET.

a public picnic or country fair. The women of the community served a huge meal at the conclusion of the military practices. In colonies to the south of New England, particularly Rhode Island, Virginia, and Maryland, horse racing, and cockfighting were often part of Muster Day.

THE GUNPOWDER PLOT

Another government-related holiday in the English colonies was Guy Fawkes Day. Guy Fawkes was a Catholic who aimed to rid England of its Protestant rulers by blowing up King James I and the Houses of Parliament on November 5, 1605. His gang of conspirators rented a cellar under the building and stuffed it with barrels of gunpowder. On November 5, as the king addressed his ministers, Fawkes planned to light the fuse and blow

▲ *An 18th-century advertisement posted in a New York newspaper before St. Patrick's Day, promising a good feast to accompany several bouts of cockfighting.*

them up. Fawkes was arrested in the cellar the night before and was tried and executed. November 5 was declared a national holiday to celebrate, and Guy Fawkes Day is still celebrated in England. Just a few years after their arrival in 1607 the settlers at Jamestown held a Guy Fawkes Day festival. Wherever it was celebrated the holiday was accompanied by bonfires, fireworks, and the burning of effigies (straw dummies) made to look like unpopular political or religious leaders. In New England the day took on decidedly anti-Catholic flavor and was called "Pope's Day." The break with Britain during the Revolutionary War meant that Guy Fawkes Day celebrations in America no longer took place.

THANKSGIVING

The first thanksgiving festival was almost certainly not celebrated by the Pilgrims, nor did it occur in the fall. In May 1578 a thanksgiving ceremony was held in Newfoundland to celebrate the safe arrival of a sailing expedition. Another thanksgiving celebration was held to celebrate the founding of the ill-fated Popham Colony in northern Virginia in 1607. However, the celebration was premature because the colony was abandoned the next year. In 1619 King James I ordered Virginians to hold an annual celebration to mark the first landing. True to his orders, the colonists set aside that day each year as a celebration until some 350 of them were massacred during a native attack in 1622 .

The Pilgrims' 1621 celebration in Plymouth was the first thanksgiving to resemble the family feasts that occur today. In the fall of that year a celebration of the successful harvest took place. By the late 17th century the type of thanksgiving day that would be recognized by Americans today was taking place. In 1665 Connecticut declared that the last Wednesday in October should be celebrated with a large family feast.

CARNIVAL AND CHRISTMAS

In French colonies the Mardi Gras festival was held on the last Tuesday before Lent (the 40-day period when Christians traditionally avoid overindulging). The words Mardi Gras mean Fat Tuesday in French. The French explorer Sieur d'Iberville first introduced Mardi Gras in 1699, but since that time the celebration has been influenced by African-American cultures. After 1718 in French-settled New Orleans Mardi Gras took on a carnival atmosphere.

Christmas festivities were frowned upon by Puritans, but many colonists still honored the holiday by either attending church or celebrating with feasting and gifts. The Dutch and the Germans introduced the feast of St. Nicholas, which they celebrated on December 6. In America St. Nicholas's day and other Christmas celebrations gradually intermixed.

All colonial Americans had special times they set aside from the normal routines of everyday life. These days were to celebrate, but also to socialize, play, and eat heartily.

SEE ALSO
FOOD AND DRINK ▥ IMMIGRATION, ENGLISH ▥ IMMIGRATION, FRENCH ▥ IMMIGRATION, GERMAN ▥ MUSIC ▥ RELIGION, NATIVE AMERICAN ▥ THANKSGIVING

F

▼ *Puritans in New England shared their celebration of thanksgiving with Native Americans.*

F FISHING

The very first explorers from Europe who sailed down the east coast of North America found rich fishing grounds of cod, mackerel, and herring in shoals so dense and deep that they seemed at times almost solidly packed together. The news generated much excitement in England, and by the beginning of the 16th century fishermen from English ports were sailing to cast their hooks and nets in the waters around Newfoundland on the far side of the Atlantic. Fishermen from England and other countries in Europe had been crossing the Atlantic for at least a century when the first of the pioneer settlers arrived to make it their permanent home.

INTERNATIONAL WATERS

Fish was in great demand among the growing populations of Europe, and the surrounding waters did not provide large enough stocks to meet this demand. The fishing banks that had been discovered off the northeast

coast of North America were therefore of great importance. The Newfoundland fishery was by far the most significant during the colonial period. Although any European nation could lawfully fish there, the fact that the English had settled on the coast of Newfoundland gave them a great advantage. Fish had to be salted, or cured, to preserve them during the long journey home. French fishermen cured their fish on board ship

◀ *A fishing community on the North Atlantic. Such settlements were not designed to be permanent and provided just basic shelters.*

◀ Fishermen set the nets for another catch. Smaller boats like these kept to the calmer, shallower waters just off the coast.

▼ Native-American tribes used a variety of ways to catch fish, including nets and spears. They tended to keep to coastal waters, inlets, and rivers.

companies also showed an interest, believing there were great profits to be made from harvesting the fish.

The growth of the fish-exporting trade was rather slow to develop, however, although it expanded more rapidly in the middle and northern colonies than in the Chesapeake Bay areas to the south.

FISHING THE SHALLOW WATERS

Although the colonists did not have many suitable vessels to risk in the hostile waters of the North Atlantic, fishing was still a very important means of survival within the first settlements. In the calmer waters of Chesapeake Bay and the rivers running into it there was a great abundance of perch, bass, and trout

between layers of salt and prepared them for market at home in France. The English filleted and cured their fish on land in a number of little settlements specially built for this purpose—the very first created by Europeans on the eastern seaboard. One of the largest customers for the cured cod was the British navy, which found it a useful source of protein during long sea voyages.

The promise of rich fisheries was a source of attraction to potential settlers, who felt assured they would not starve with the North Atlantic so close at hand. The English government and commercial

F

that provided food for local people. Sturgeon—large sharklike fish that swim upriver to lay their eggs—were also regularly caught by fishermen using canoes similar to those of the Native Americans.

THE HARVEST OF THE SEA

The first center for commercial deep-sea fishing in colonial America was Salem, Massachusetts. It is believed that the first ship was built here in 1624 by a carpenter from England. It was most probably a "shallop"—a type of small, open boat with both a sail and oars. In the later part of the 17th century sturdier ships were built to fish the Grand Banks of Newfoundland, and by the 1670s there were fleets of several hundred boats catching cod and herring. The best quality fish went to Spain and Portugal, the second grade to the Canary Islands and Madeira, and the poorest was sent to the Caribbean as slave food.

▲ *Shellfish such as lobsters, caught off the rocky shores of New England, became an important part of the area's economy and the settlers' diet.*

CURING COD

By the middle of the 18th century, when this woodcut was produced, salt cod production was a highly efficient industry. Fishing was either by net or by a weighted hook and line, as held by the fisherman in the foreground. His warm sealskin coat provided protection from the harsh climate in Newfoundland. The people on the timber pier in the background are gutting the fish. The cod were then salted in large troughs and finally laid out to dry on the tables in the foreground.

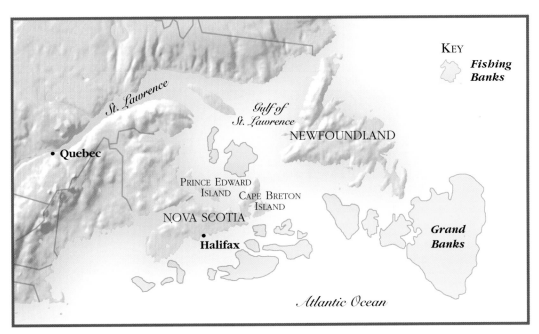

◀ *The northeast coast of North America had a number of areas rich in fish. The Grand Banks were the largest.*

▼ *A French fishing fleet at the Grand Banks. In early spring, before the fishing season, many fishermen traveled north to hunt seals.*

In an attempt to control the growth of the commercial sea-fishing industry in the 18th century the British government banned the export of salt to the Chesapeake region. The aim was to prevent the spread of the industry to the South, where the government wanted people to grow valuable crops such as tobacco.

AN UNPOPULAR MOVE

In defiance of the ban on salt George Washington began a successful fishery on the Potomac River in 1760. In return for his barrels of salted herring Washington got rum, coffee, sugar, and oranges from the West Indies. The ban on salt angered him a great deal and was one of the many reasons he fought for freedom from the British.

Later, as the Revolutionary War began, the English tried to ban the colonies' export of fish altogether in order to undermine their economy, but the crews of the American fishing fleets fought to continue their trans-Atlantic trade.

SEE ALSO

NEWFOUNDLAND ■ TRADE ■ WASHINGTON, GEORGE ■ WEST INDIES

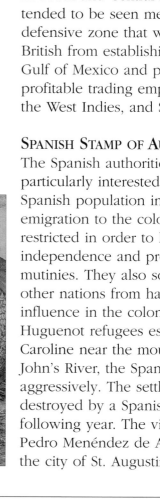

FLORIDA

Though it was settled earlier than most other colonies, Florida remained an undeveloped outpost of Spain's South and Central American Empire through most of the colonial period. The territory was first claimed for Spain by the explorer Juan Ponce de León, who made landfall near the present-day city of St. Augustine in the spring of 1513. Ponce de León named the new territory after the Easter festival, *pascua florida* in Spanish, and was appointed as the first governor of Florida in 1514. He died there during an attack by natives in 1521. The natives that León would have met in Florida during the 16th century, such as the Calusa, had come from a variety of regions, including Cuba and the Bahamas. By the 18th century, however, most of these had been wiped out by Europeans and by Creek natives from Georgia. The Creek who stayed in the area evolved into the family known as the Seminole.

The Spanish never really attempted to colonize Florida by establishing permanent settlements; they were too busy shipping back gold and other

▶ *Fort Caroline was built on the Florida coast by French settlers in 1564. Many of the Protestant settlers had experienced religious persecution in their homeland. The Spanish, however, destroyed the settlement within a year.*

▼ *This engraving of Florida natives battling with impossibly large alligators dates from the 1590s. It was war, disease, and slave traders, however, that led to the natives' disappearance.*

treasures looted during their conquests in South and Central America. Florida tended to be seen merely as a defensive zone that would prevent the British from establishing a port on the Gulf of Mexico and protect Spain's profitable trading empire in Mexico, the West Indies, and South America.

SPANISH STAMP OF AUTHORITY

The Spanish authorities were not particularly interested in increasing the Spanish population in Florida, and emigration to the colonies was restricted in order to limit economic independence and prevent potential mutinies. They also sought to prevent other nations from having any influence in the colony. When French Huguenot refugees established Fort Caroline near the mouth of the St. John's River, the Spanish reacted aggressively. The settlement was destroyed by a Spanish fleet the following year. The victorious admiral, Pedro Menéndez de Avilés, founded the city of St. Augustine in 1565. This

F

was the first permanent European settlement in North America, built as a defensive base against further settlers.

During the following two centuries Spain's strategy was not to launch direct attacks against British and French settlements, but rather to generate unrest among the Native-American population in the Carolinas, Georgia, and Louisiana, and to encourage slaves to escape from English plantations. In the 18th century the Spanish mission of Gracia Real de Santa Teresa de Mose, near St. Augustine, offered freedom and land to any escaped slave who became a Roman Catholic. In 1740, after two years' existence, the mission was destroyed when a fleet led by James Oglethorpe besieged St. Augustine.

Florida remained the northern outpost of the Spanish Empire until the British victory in the French and Indian War, which Spain entered in 1761. In 1763 the Treaty of Paris transferred the colony to the British, who split it into two districts, East and West Florida, with the Appalachicola and Chattahoochee Rivers as the boundaries. Many of the 3,000 Spanish settlers sold up and went south to Cuba and Mexico. During their occupation the British were largely confined to small military settlements at St. Augustine in the east and Pensacola and St. Marks in the west.

The Floridas became a haven for Loyalists at the beginning of the Revolutionary War, although St. Augustine fell to the Patriots and Pensacola to Spanish troops from New Orleans in 1781. The aid given by Spain in the war was recognized in the Treaty of Paris in 1783, which restored Florida to Spanish control.

SEE ALSO
FRENCH AND INDIAN WAR ■ IMMIGRATION, FRENCH ■ LOYALISTS ■ NEW SPAIN ■ OGLETHORPE, JAMES ■ ST. AUGUSTINE ■ TREATY OF PARIS, 1783

▼ *A palm-lined street in the settlement of St. Augustine. Built as a defense against British and French colonists, the troubled town was ransacked by Francis Drake in 1585 and by James Oglethorpe in 1740.*

F FOOD AND DRINK

▲ *Borrowing techniques and ingredients from the Native Americans helped the first settlers survive in their unfamiliar land. These natives are drying fish and other wild animals to preserve the meat for future use.*

Although the first Puritan English settlers in North America might have been shocked by the Native Americans' seminudity and seemingly primitive customs, they soon found themselves adopting some of their ways of farming and eating.

The colonists were at first unfamiliar with the Native Americans' methods of farming and with the main crop they produced—corn. The Native Americans were skillful cultivators of the land, planting corn in rows and growing it together with beans and squash. The settlers soon learned to cultivate these crops, which they had never come across before, and adapt them to their diet. Corn came to be as important to the

Europeans as it was to the native people and undoubtedly helped fend off starvation for the poorer farmers during the harsh winters.

The pilgrims might have adapted the staple crops of the Native Americans, but they retained many European farming practices. The colonists were more familiar with domesticated animals such as cattle and sheep and did not encourage wild animals onto their land. The Native Americans, however, liked the native grasses to grow so that deer and other wild animals could graze.

English settlers in the most prosperous colonies—Massachusetts and Virginia in particular—also tended to eat and drink as they had in their mother country and still appreciated their coffee, tea, and the foods they had eaten at home—finely sliced buttered bread, shavings of ham and beef, jams, floury muffins, fruits, and pistachios and other nuts. The wealthiest settlers ate and drank these delicacies from English china tea sets.

ONE-POT GOODNESS

The poorer farmers and artisans and their families, however, saw more of earthenware pots and wooden bowls than fine china. Their lifestyle was not luxurious, and only at Thanksgiving and religious festivals would they have enjoyed such treats.

Poorer families relied largely on the "one-pot" meal. The midday meal, the most important meal of the day, was usually supplied from a large pot of stew, a nourishing concoction of meat and vegetables. One of the most popular one-pot meals was Boston Baked Beans. Although it was a simple recipe, it became the staple weekend feast for the humbler Massachusetts families and has been a

part of the culture of New England ever since. White beans were slowly simmered in an earthenware pot with ham, pork slices, and brown sugar. The rich, tasty stew was eaten with thick slices of brown molasses bread.

It was unusual for alcohol to be served with meals at the family dinner table. Sometimes a glass of home-brewed beer might be served, but only for the men—women rarely indulged in alcohol. Milk, soft cider, fruit juices, and an occasional cordial accompanied meals.

The men of the colonies tended to keep their wine, cider, beer, and spirit drinking to taverns. Evenings were spent playing darts and skittles and drinking from foaming tankards of beer. Records show that in 1737 there were 177 taverns in Boston, and in 1752 New York had 334.

Among the upper classes, in Virginia, for example, the richer men got together in large halls and mansions to celebrate great events. In September 1716, after the successful expedition of General Alexander

▼ A Massachusetts farmhouse tavern as it looked in the mid-18th century. This is the kitchen, where food was prepared. Drinks were served in a separate bar room.

F Spotswood's regiment to the Shenandoah Valley, members of his troop met for a celebratory meal and consumed a large amount of alcohol: "We had a good dinner...and we drunk the King's health in Champagne...and all the rest of the Royal Family in claret...We drunk the Governor's health and fired a volley. We had several sort of liquors, namely Virginia Red Wine and white wine, Irish Usquebaugh [whiskey], Brandy, two sorts of Rum, Champagne, Canary, Cherry Punch, Cider, Water, etc."

It is interesting to note that this banquet included the serving of "Virginia Red" wine. Early settlers discovered that the eastern seaboard was alive with lush wild grapes, and during the first hundred years the colonists struggled to make wine from cultivated grapes. Unfortunately, this industry never thrived in the east; the landowners blamed the salt that blew

▶ *The kitchen of the Shirley plantation, the earliest Virginia slave plantation.*

▼ *An oysterman selling his wares in Philadelphia. The Atlantic seaboard offered a plentiful supply of fish and shellfish.*

in from the Atlantic. Undaunted by the failures, William Penn, the founder of Pennsylvania, experimented with growing French vines and also sampled some native varieties, which he pronounced "good claret" grapes, but his attempts at viticulture (the growing of grapes) enjoyed little success. However, one of the products of the industry, grape juice, became a national passion. By the 19th century there was a large market for juices made from berries such as cranberries and blackberries and tree fruits such as apples and peaches.

FOOD AND FESTIVALS

The English colonists still celebrated many of their traditional religious feast-days, such as the wheat-harvest festival of August 1. This festival was similar to the Thanksgiving Day now celebrated in November in the U.S. On this day people gave thanks to the Lord for helping them survive in the New World and for providing all the foodstuffs that kept them alive, such as wild turkeys, sweet potatoes, corn, and pumpkins.

Dutch settlers in New York also tended to keep up the customs, including mealtimes and recipes, of their homeland, although they were also willing to adapt to new foodstuffs. A typical day's meals began with breakfast, generally served at 7:00 AM and consisting of tea with milk, bread and butter, slices of dried beef and ham, and grated cheese. For the midday meal they had milk or buttermilk and bread, along with roasted meat and a salad served with vinegar. Supper was usually a simple meal of bread in milk or porridge made of cornmeal similar to the Native-American dish *sappan*.

By the mid-17th century both the northern and southern colonies had come to rely on these types of corn-based meals. In the Spanish borderlands—Texas, New Mexico, Florida—a cornmeal gruel, called *atole*, was a staple food. In the same period the more affluent southern settlers of the Carolinas discovered the joys of cornbread loaves and muffins, which are still a favorite in the southern states. Colonists were also

taught an effective way to roast meat on a frame over a bed of charcoal, known as a *barbacoa* by the Native Americans—the forerunner of the barbecue that is still so popular today.

ADDING A LITTLE SPICE
Herbs and spices have long been used to disguise and improve the flavor of poor-quality meat. Settlers in the colonies were introduced to a new selection of flavorings traditionally used by the natives. The hunters in the Spanish borderlands made the most of what food was available to them: raccoon, squirrel, and beaver all formed part of their diet. To make

▲ *Drinking tea had become enormously popular in 18th-century Britain, and the colonists brought the habit to America with them. When Parliament dared to interfere with tea imports, the colonists' reaction led to the Boston Tea Party.*

F

▶ *The turkey was a wild bird popular with Native Americans when the first settlers arrived. It is now farmed and eaten all over North America and is the traditional centerpiece for the Thanksgiving dinner.*

them taste better they used a technique that is common all over the world: they added spices, in this case using the red chili spice popular with the local natives. In Louisiana the French settlers also added flavor to their food with hot spices, using a native blend that contains cayenne pepper, now known as Cajun spices.

FOOD FROM THE WILD

The French also learned ways of preserving fish and game from the Timucua natives of northeast Florida. In Quebec the French settlers took lessons from the Native Americans on how to trap, prepare, and cook a variety of forest animals. In one old French-Canadian recipe book for squirrel stew the directions are very basic: "Skin squirrels and clean good, removing all hairs."

In exchange, Europeans provided the native population with some useful ideas. In 1769, for example, Hector St. John de Crèvecoeur, a French settler in Canada, introduced European crops such as alfalfa, which is used as cattle feed.

▼ *Pumpkins, squashes, and related vegetables such as cucumbers were unknown in Europe in the 17th century.*

One of the most popular products introduced both to the colonists and to Europe was cocoa. Chocolate, made from cocoa beans, had been popular among the Aztecs in Mexico for centuries and was brought to the coffee houses of America and Europe by a Dominican monk, Thomas Gage. He excitedly reported finding it in Mexico in 1648 and warned fanciers that "this chocolattical confection... could provoke sleeplessness."

The best-fed colonists were usually the ones who were willing to experiment with their food. French settlers in Louisiana created many recipes from local produce that are still popular today, and generations of New Englanders have made good use of the crabs, clams, lobsters, and shrimp that surround their shores. Their mouthwatering chowders and clambakes continue to attract food lovers from all over the world.

SEE ALSO

FARMING ■ FESTIVALS ■ FISHING ■ THANKSGIVING

FORESTRY

Many of the settlers who came to the east coast of North America dreamed of finding gold in the vast, unconquered territory, but very few of their dreams ever came true. There were other, unexpected riches to be had from the land, however. The French made fortunes from furs, while many of the English plantation owners grew rich from growing tobacco and indigo. Others looked to the vast forests that covered the land and saw the chance to make their fortunes in the harvest of timber.

CONTROLLED CLEARANCE

Contrary to popular belief, the eastern seaboard was not a vast wilderness of thick forests. Clearings and grassland prairies within the forests were abundant. Some were the result of natural soil differences, while others came from the hands of Native Americans. They had learned to cultivate the forests by carefully burning certain areas in order to encourage game animals to graze on the fields of grass that later grew.

The forests represented both challenge and opportunity, and different cultures brought different ideas on how to cope with uncleared land. The Scots-Irish of Ulster, a land which had been almost stripped bare of timber by the needs of the British navy, continued this pattern of destruction in America. They "girdled" trees by removing circular bands of bark from around the trunks. Unable to transport nutrients from the roots to the leaves, the trees dropped their leaves and then slowly died. In the meantime, crops were planted around the leafless trees.

SKILLED MANAGEMENT

The study of forestry was first developed in Central Europe, and immigrants from this area generally showed a greater respect for the environment. Forests and the animals living within them were carefully

The gold of an autumn forest may not have been the treasure sought by the first explorers, but the trees of North America still proved to be a valuable resource.

F

managed by professional foresters. German-speaking farmers brought this tradition of forestry to America. In Pennsylvania in particular many of their farms contained neat, managed woodlots. These woodlots, usually consisting of hardwood trees like oak and hickory, formed a renewable resource that could be harvested and replanted over a period of years.

The English had a mixed attitude to forestry. The Irish landscape had been exploited by generations of English landowners, but in some English counties woodland was properly cultivated in woodlots to provide saplings that could be used to make woven fences and wall panels for houses. It was the English, however, who spearheaded the exploitation of timber resources in the New World by offering bounties or cash bonuses paid to those who exported forest products to England.

Much of the demand came from the British navy, which needed huge quantities of lumber for building ships. There was also a constant need

Little thought went into the clearance of most forests. Instead of selective harvesting, which leaves some trees behind to preserve the forest environment, workers simply removed every tree from the area, leaving the land unprotected.

for by-products of the lumber industry such as tar, pitch, resin, and turpentine. These thick, sticky substances are known collectively as naval stores. They were all obtained from pine trees and used to waterproof and seal everything on a ship—from the cracks between boards to the ropes and sails. The English thought that if they could produce enough naval stores in their own colonies, they could eliminate the need to import them from the countries around the Baltic Sea in northern Europe.

PRODUCTS OF PINE

The production of most naval stores depended on the harvest of conifers, or needle-bearing trees, like pines and spruce. As early as 1608 the settlers at Jamestown were experimenting with making tar and pitch from longleaf pine trees. This industry existed until long after the Revolutionary War and resulted in the destruction of much of the longleaf pine forest found in the south. From 1727 until 1749 Virginia exported 10,000 barrels of pitch and tar every year.

Naval stores were also of great economic importance in Georgia, South Carolina, North Carolina, Florida, and Louisiana. In South

Wooden ships were the only way to transport goods and people between Europe and the colonies. This, together with the needs of Britain's navy, meant there was a constant demand for timber for shipbuilding. Most of the ships were built in the colonies—little timber was exported.

Carolina planters used the timber industry as a way to keep their workers busy in the winter when there were no crops to harvest. In North Carolina farmers harvested pine from their own small farms.

Many other products could be produced from the seemingly endless North American forests. At that time people were heavily dependent on wood for uses such as cooking, heating, houses, wagons and carriages, furniture, and fencing. Wooden barrels were used for holding everything from flour, fish, wine, tobacco, and apples to turpentine, tar, and pitch. As a consequence, a businessman could always make money by producing barrel staves (the long wooden ribs of the barrel), for which there was always a demand.

A USE FOR EVERY TREE
Nearly every type of tree was harvested and used. Barrel staves were often made of oak. Weather-resistant cedar and cypress trees were used to make roof shingles, while mahogany, walnut, maple, and oak were turned into furniture.

In Georgia, rather than concentrate on the production of tar and pitch for naval stores, laborers turned timber into staves, roof shingles, and building lumber. Free lumber workers earned enough during the winter months to support themselves for the entire year. In Louisiana's pine forests slaves were put to work making tar and pitch, while in forested areas destined for growing other crops slaves were told to clear the trees and turn them into board lumber.

The timber industry flourished in nearly every colony. In New York, however, it got off to a rocky start. A group of 3,000 Germans was transported to the colony for the purpose of producing naval stores so

A northern logging camp. The tall, straight pines of the northern colonies were ideal for building simple log cabins.

they could pay off the cost of their passage to America. Unfortunately, nearly 800 of the potential workers died during the journey, and the enterprise failed within two years.

THE LAUNCH OF SHIPBUILDING
The Massachusetts shipbuilding industry was a far greater success. Shipbuilders in the Massachusetts Bay Colony launched the first seafaring vessel, *The Blessing of the Bay,* in 1631, and over the next 150 years a great number of boats and ships were produced in New England shipyards. At the time of the Revolutionary War one-third of the ships in the British navy had been built in North America. The tall, straight, white pines that grew in New England were prized by the British navy for ships' masts.

Many forestry practices in colonial America were destructive of the environment. Lumber workers simply cut down entire areas of timber and then moved on to the next forest with little or no thought for replanting the trees. By the time the Revolutionary War began many places along the east coast were already suffering from shortages of wood.

SEE ALSO

FARMING ■ IMMIGRATION, GERMAN ■ IMMIGRATION, SCOTS-IRISH ■ JAMESTOWN ■ MASSACHUSETTS ■ TRADE

WOODWORK

*N*orth American colonists perfected a number of methods for producing naval stores, which involved highly specialized tools. Turpentine was harvested by cutting into pine trees with a broadax, a maul, or a pringle ax to make them secrete a sticky, gumlike substance: a process known as chipping. At the next stage six-foot (2-m) slices were cut at angles into the trunk of the trees. The slice was made with either a long-handled puller or the shorter hack, depending on the height of the cut. The gum ran down gutters inserted into the slices and was collected in containers called cups that were place at the point where the cuts met.

Workers, often slaves, collected the turpentine into barrels. Two and a half barrels could be collected every day from 1,000 trees. Once collected, the liquid was distilled, or heated, to burn off the impurities. The result was a clear, colorless liquid used in paints and varnishes. A by-product of distilling turpentine is resin, used in making varnish. Turpentine was gathered from the same trees once every two weeks during the summer. The gum eventually hardened over the incisions in the trunk and had to be removed with a scraper. Although the process did not kill the tree, it damaged it enough to make it vulnerable to disease and harsh weather.

Tar, another of the products of the colonial forest industry, is a thick, black, sticky liquid produced by burning pine wood. Further heating of tar in big kettles produces a more refined product called pitch. Both are used on rope to make it rot-resistant. Sticky black tar and pitch are also used to seal the seams in ships and make them watertight.

BENJAMIN FRANKLIN

B en Franklin was one of America's greatest statesmen as well as a printer, publisher, writer, philosopher, diplomat, and scientist. One of the most famous and most respected international figures of the 18th century, he was dubbed "the first civilized American."

Born in Boston on January 17, 1706, Franklin was third youngest of 17 children. His father, a candle- and soap-maker, taught him to read, but the young Franklin showed an early desire to become a sailor, much to his father's disapproval. After training as a cutlery maker, at the age of 12 he became an apprentice to his brother James who had recently brought a printing press from London.

EARLY IMPRESSIONS

While learning the printing trade, Franklin educated himself by reading a wide range of books. Franklin was so inspired by a volume of the British journal *The Spectator* that he learned its essays by heart to try to master their style.

In 1721 Franklin's brother James set up a liberal newspaper called the *New England Courant* to which Franklin contributed many articles. The paper was highly critical of local government and religious authorities. This landed its proprietor in jail in 1722, during which time Benjamin continued to publish the paper.

After a disagreement with his brother Ben Franklin left Boston for Philadelphia. He arrived there in October 1723 and was soon befriended by Pennsylvania's

▲ *Benjamin Franklin inspects the first edition of the* Pennsylvania Gazette *produced under his editorship. As a writer, Franklin sometimes used the name Richard Saunders.*

Governor, Sir William Keith. He convinced Franklin to go to London to continue training as a printer. Franklin took his advice, and though Keith's promised financial support never appeared, he quickly found work with one of London's best printers. In 1726 Franklin returned to Philadelphia and continued in the printing trade.

During the following year he formed a group known as Junto—the Spanish word *junta* means a society for political discussion—to debate moral, philosophical, and political issues. Junto proposed such civic-minded projects as improved street paving, street lighting, a paid police force, and a volunteer fire corps, all of which were eventually adopted. Junto formed the basis of the American Philosophical Society.

In 1729 Franklin bought a dull weekly paper, the *Pennsylvania Gazette*, and turned it into a witty and informative newspaper. The following year he had a son with his common-

F

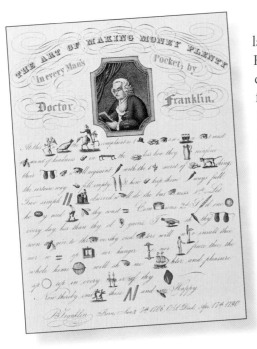

The first line of this puzzle written by Franklin reads, "At this time when the major complaint is that money is so scarce it must be an act of kindness to instruct the moneyless how they can reinforce their wallets…"

law wife Deborah Read, but the boy died at the age of four. His daughter Sarah and William, his illegitimate son from a previous relationship, were also brought up in the household. In 1732 he published an extremely successful series of books called *Poor Richard's Almanacs* based on ancient proverbs, but throughout the next two decades Franklin's main areas of focus were politics, philanthropy (concerned with the welfare of the human race), and science.

A MAN OF MANY PARTS

Franklin became a member of the St. John's Lodge in 1731, believed to be one of the first of the secret societies known as the Freemasons. That same year he founded America's first subscription library, which eventually became the Philadelphia Library. Franklin was involved with politics from an early age. At the age of 30, in 1736, he became clerk of the Pennsylvania General Assembly, and in 1737 he was appointed Deputy Postmaster of Philadelphia, a post which he held until 1753, when he became one of the two deputy postmasters general for the colonies.

Franklin continued to pursue his interest in science. In 1749 he wrote *Proposals Relating to the Education of Youth in Pennsylvania* and founded the Philadelphia Academy to provide training in the arts and sciences. The academy opened in 1751.

In the 1740s Franklin began experimenting with electricity, and in

1752 he proved that lightning is created by an electrical charge. He was a member of scientific societies in Europe and Russia and was also awarded honorary degrees from such universities as Harvard, Yale, Edinburgh, and Oxford in recognition of his scientific studies. Geology, chemistry, physiology (the study of living matter), psychology, and hydrology (the study of water) were further areas of scientific interest.

In 1748 Franklin retired from printing and decided to concentrate on politics. In 1750 he was elected to the Pennsylvania Assembly, and four years later he became Pennsylvania's delegate to the Albany Congress, which debated ways of dealing with the impending French and Indian War. He played an important role in raising funds for the defense of Pennsylvania and spent a great deal of time in England between 1757 and 1762 negotiating a system of taxation to pay for the war.

In 1723 Franklin arrived in Philadelphia penniless, with little more than a loaf of bread to sustain him.

F

organize a postal system and attempted, unsuccessfully, to convince Canada to fight against the British. He also contributed to the draft of the Declaration of Independence.

In September 1776 Franklin was sent with Arthur Lee to join Silas Deane in Paris to try and win military and economic assistance from the French. Franklin managed to persuade the French to supply around 12,000 soldiers, 32,000 sailors, and substantial loans of money. Within the year Franklin was appointed by Congress as America's ambassador to France.

After the defeat of the British forces at Yorktown in October 1781 Franklin, along with John Adams and John Jay, began peace negotiations with Britain. On September 3, 1783, the Treaty of Paris was signed, ending the war. Though Franklin asked to return to America, Congress felt he was essential for the negotiation of crucial trade treaties, and he was persuaded to remain in France.

Franklin returned to Philadelphia in September 1785 suffering from gallstones, but despite his illness he was appointed president of the Pennsylvania Council. During his term in office as a delegate to the Constitutional Convention, he helped draw up the U.S. Constitution.

On April 17, 1790, Benjamin Franklin died at home in Philadelphia. He is remembered as a great diplomat, a wise and witty speaker, and a much loved and respected statesman who truly represented the spirit of the New World.

Franklin remained in London till 1762, then again from 1764 to 1775, representing the American colonies. His diplomatic skills were stretched in the effort to explain the grievances of the colonies. In 1766 he helped get the despised Stamp Act repealed, but he still believed in the possibility of a British empire of self-governing colonies that formed a kind of commonwealth. During this time Franklin was befriended by such eminent figures as the economist Adam Smith.

In 1775 Franklin returned to America, convinced that war could not be avoided. He arrived on May 5, 1775, discovering that the battles of Lexington and Concord had already been fought. The following day he was appointed as a delegate to the Second Continental Congress convened on May 10. Here he helped

▲ *Franklin is shown here "capturing electricity from the heavens" in the type of romanticized and heroic pose that was favored by portrait artists in the late 18th century.*

SEE ALSO

FREE BLACKS

Not all blacks living in colonial America were slaves, but hardly any of them had come to the continent as willing immigrants. In the early 1700s the status of Africans in colonial America was difficult to define, and Europeans' attitudes to slaves varied. Slavery did not exist in England, although the Spanish and Portuguese had been taking West Africans to work as forced labor in the baking heat of South American and West Indian plantations since the early years of the 16th century.

THE CHANCE OF FREEDOM

At first, African servants had roughly the same status as white indentured servants; both could be bought and sold, they were often housed together, and they sometimes escaped together. Black people had rights that would later be denied them under the slave codes: they were allowed to own and to inherit property, and could take out lawsuits and have them heard in the courts. They could also become free men; some were granted their freedom in return for hard work, faithful service, or cash payments, while others were freed in their master's will. Sometimes they were given a plot of land, too.

As the tobacco industry expanded, the demand for labor on the plantations of Virginia and Maryland increased. From the 1660s the colonies passed harsh laws aimed at keeping in slavery for life any Africans who had not already been granted their freedom. Plantation owners could punish those who rebelled or broke any rules. Slaves could still buy or be given their freedom in some of the New England colonies, however.

By 1760 there were probably no more than 2,000 free blacks in Virginia out of a total black population of 340,000, although there was a sizable free black community in Williamsburg. In South Carolina, which strictly enforced a law requiring any slave who was freed to leave the colony, the number of free blacks in 1760 was even smaller: just 200–300 people, about 1 percent of the total.

In the northern colonies the proportion of free blacks was higher—maybe one in 10 north of Maryland—but their numbers were just as low because the black populations were much lower. The total black population of Connecticut,

▲ A black servant from a wealthy household. By the time this picture was painted in 1770 blacks had very few rights and very little freedom.

CRISPUS ATTUCKS

Crispus Attucks, a free black, was the first person to fall in the Boston Massacre of 1770 (he is shown in the picture below, on the right). Little is known of his origins; he is thought to have been a slave who was advertised as a runaway in 1750 and to have spent much of the next 20 years as a sailor on whaling ships. On March 5 Attucks was at the head of a mob that assaulted the British soldiers and provoked them to fire. Five people were shot down and killed, including Attucks.

for example, was only 2,000, although 400 of them were free.

Freedom did not bring equality with whites for the majority of blacks in America. In Virginia, for example, free blacks could no longer vote after 1723, serve in the militia, or own guns and could not testify against whites in court. This meant that even those who became relatively prosperous were not secure from threats, bullying, and even being kidnapped back into

slavery. The northern colonies were no better. In New York free blacks were forbidden to own real estate. Even in Massachusetts, well-known for its liberal politics, blacks were denied the vote, and marriages between blacks were not recognized by law.

THE PROBLEMS OF FREEDOM

The major problem for free blacks, though, especially in the South, was earning a living. Discrimination made it virtually impossible to buy property, although some became tenant farmers. Laboring work—the only option open to most—was difficult to come by; and when work did turn up, it was usually very hard and poorly paid. Although some blacks had trained as carpenters or blacksmiths when they were slaves, they found it difficult to work in such trades outside Williamsburg and a few other towns. White tradesmen did not allow them to compete for work.

Some free blacks, particularly those with large families, grew weary of the struggle and were forced back into servitude, if not outright slavery. Although the children of freedmen were free themselves, the problem of supporting them was a great burden.

More slaves were freed in the Revolutionary War when the British occupied the southern colonies. Although 5,000 black men fought for the Patriots, most of them were free blacks from the northern states. The majority of free blacks involved in the conflict fought on the Loyalist side, however, and thousands of black Loyalists sailed out of the new United States with the British Army in 1783.

SEE ALSO

BOSTON MASSACRE ▪ CONNECTICUT ▪ MASSACHUSETTS ▪ PLANTATIONS ▪ SLAVE TRADE ▪ SLAVERY ▪ SOUTH CAROLINA ▪ VIRGINIA ▪ WILLIAMSBURG

F FRENCH AND INDIAN WAR

The French and Indian War that took place between 1754 and 1763 was the final war between the British and French for control of the New World. By 1756 the battle had spread to Europe and taken in Spain and Portugal as well as several German states. They were all battling for domination of central Europe in what became known as the Seven Years' War and which took place between 1756 and 1763.

A CONFLICT OF INTERESTS

The French and Indian War began as a conflict over control of the Ohio Valley. The valley is in an ideal position within the larger valley of the Mississippi. Both sides in the dispute knew the importance of the valley, since it marks the beginning of the interior of North America. The British claim to the region rested on John Cabot's discovery of North America in the 15th century and on a royal charter in the early 17th century that granted all the land between the Atlantic and Pacific oceans to Virginia and the Grand Council for New England. In 1682 the French explorer René-Robert Cavelier, Sieur de La Salle claimed for France all the lands drained by the Mississippi River and its tributaries during his exploration of the area.

By the middle of the 18th century British traders were venturing into the disputed Ohio Valley to trade with Native Americans who had previously dealt only with the French. Tensions between the two nations increased during the 1740s when a Virginia land-speculating firm, the Ohio Company, tried to establish a settlement at the point where the Monongahela and

Allegheny Rivers meet to form the Ohio River—the site of present-day Pittsburgh, Pennsylvania.

Native-American warriors were recruited by both sides, which supplied them with arms and stirred up trouble between opposing tribes. At the beginning of the conflict most of the native tribes took the side of the French, who had established good relations with them throughout the previous century. The British did make various alliances with the Iroquois, who conducted raids against

▲ *An Iroquois warrior during the French and Indian War. The end of his musket is decorated with a scalp, for which he could have been paid a reward by the British.*

The French fort at Ticonderoga. British forces under General Abercrombie attempted to storm the well-defended fort on July 6, 1758. Over 2,000 of them died in the assault.

French settlements and fought in many of the major battles, but there were regular disagreements between the two sides, and a large number of Iroquois changed their allegiance.

To protect his colony's fur-trading interests, in 1749 the French governor general of Canada ordered the explorer Pierre Joseph de Blainville to claim the Ohio Valley for France and remove the British trespassers. There was much bloodshed as the French and their Native-American allies carried out their orders, looting the

British settlements and murdering the inhabitants. In 1753 the French began to construct a line of forts from Lake Erie to the start of the Ohio River. Virginia's Governor Robert Dinwiddie retaliated the following year by sending an army under George Washington to expel the French from the valley. On July 4, 1754, Washington's troops were defeated in the battle of Fort Necessity.

When news of Washington's defeat reached London, Parliament responded by sending two regiments to the colonies under the command of General Edward Braddock. In a clear attempt to finally remove the French from Ohio they also ordered New England settlers to attack French settlements in New France. For the first four years of the war the French were far more successful, defeating General Braddock's army as it attempted to take Fort Duquesne on

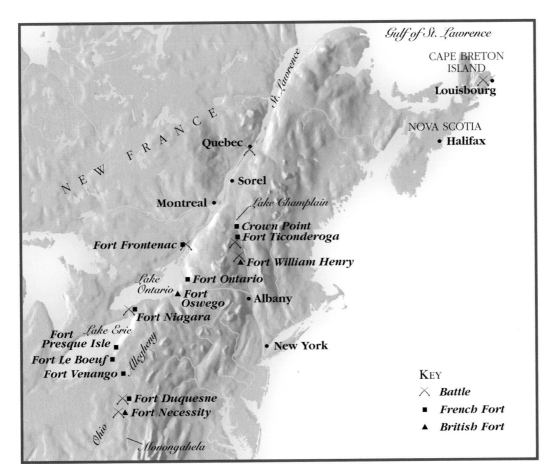

The major battles of the French and Indian War. Settlements in the French colonies relied heavily on inland waterways for transport and communication. Whoever controlled the rivers controlled the northern territories.

F the Ohio River in 1755. Braddock died in the battle and was replaced by Lord Loudon, who was despatched to North America with a further two regiments of regular soldiers, indicating the increasing importance which the British attached to the conflict. He arrived too late to prevent the Marquis de Montcalm from capturing Fort Oswego on Lake Ontario, a vitally important British trading post.

ALL-OUT WAR

It was obvious that the British tactics were not working, and Loudon decided to make a direct assault on the center of French power on the St. Lawrence River. To achieve his aim, Loudon requested a further 10,000 troops from Britain. By concentrating on the vital supply lines between France and the colonies, the British were able to cut off New France from essential supplies of food, ammunition, and reinforcements. The battle on the mainland was less successful, and on August 3, 1757, Fort William Henry near Lake Champlain fell to Montcalm's troop. The new British government under Prime Minister William Pitt promised

victory to the British people. Pitt recognized that with the spread of the French and Indian War to other parts of the world, victory in North America was essential. He sent his best officers, recruited new soldiers, and calmed the colonists by offering to reimburse them for any losses they suffered during the war. The British navy then fought to gain supremacy in the North Atlantic.

In June of 1758 the tide of the war began to turn in favor of Britain, when a British force under General Amherst captured Louisbourg on Cape Breton Island, inflicting heavy casualties on the French defenders. General Abercrombie's attempt later in the year to take Fort Ticonderoga was a costly failure, however, and 2,000

▲ *In the spring of 1763 the Ottawa tribe, led by their chief Pontiac, laid siege to the British fort of Detroit. Pontiac was a great leader but was unable to capture Detroit.*

▼ *In 1755 combined forces of French soldiers and their native allies defeated the British at Fort Duquesne and shot dead General Braddock.*

British and colonial troops were killed. Despite the setback the British became more determined than ever to capture all of the French territories.

The decisive battle of the French and Indian War was fought at Quebec, the most important city in New France at the time. This was part of a larger campaign against French positions at Ticonderoga, Crown Point, and Niagara. After sailing up the St. Lawrence in a fleet of small boats, British troops under General James Wolfe scaled the steep cliffs from the river during the night and surprised the French in Quebec. Both Wolfe and the French commander Montcalm were killed in the battle, which was a comprehensive British victory.

THE FINAL ASSAULT

During the fall of 1759 the famous raid by Rogers's Rangers on the native settlement of St. Francis took place. Robert Rogers, a major in the British army, marched with a force of his men across enemy territory to the village, located near Sorel on the St. Lawrence River. On the morning of October 6 they attacked. Very few of the tribal warriors were around to defend the settlement, and the troops massacred many of the native women and children as they tried to escape.

In 1760 William Pitt ordered preparations for a final campaign to be made. Throughout the year the three British armies fought their way toward Montreal. On September 7, realizing his position was hopeless, the governor general of Montreal, the Marquis de Vaudreuil, surrendered Canada's last stronghold to the British.

▶ *Rogers's Rangers making their exhausting march to St. Francis. Rogers was one of the popular heroes of the war but was tried for treason in 1768 and died in poverty in London in 1795.*

This surrender ended the North American phase of the Seven Years' War, although fighting continued in Europe and the Caribbean.

In the final peace treaty signed in Paris in 1763 France gave up virtually all its North American claims to Britain. The scale of the victory actually sowed the seeds for Britain's later destruction in America. In winning the French and Indian War, Britain acquired more land than it was capable of governing, and in the effort to support this huge territory it antagonized the colonies by imposing taxes on them. With Britain having cleared the continent of many of the colonies' enemies, they no longer needed the motherland and had no desire to submit to British taxes or authority. Furthermore, France, having been humiliated by Britain, was a willing ally when the colonies decided to separate from Britain in the Revolutionary War that was to follow a decade later.

SEE ALSO

▲ *The British produced this commemorative medal for their native allies although the Native Americans received little other reward for their support.*

F | COMPTE LOUIS DE FRONTENAC

Compte Louis de Frontenac was born in St. Germain, France, in 1622. He entered into a career in the French army, and although he reached the equivalent rank of brigadier general by 1646, he was corrupt and notoriously extravagant and ran up huge debts. In 1672 Frontenac was appointed governor of New France. His attempts to take over the powers of the *intendant*, the government official in charge of the economy of the colony, annoyed the authorities in France, who promptly reduced his political powers. Turning his attentions to the expanding fur trade, he established the trading post of Fort Frontenac on Lake Ontario, as well as trading posts on Lake Michigan and the Illinois River. This French expansion into the Great Lakes territories greatly angered the native Iroquois tribes, who largely controlled the western fur trade.

FIGHTING FOR FURS
Frontenac's mismanagement of the colony led to his recall to France in 1682. Seven years later, however, after a number of Iroquois attacks in New France, he was once again appointed governor. Aided by native tribes, Frontenac led raids against the New England frontier settlements, prompting the British colonies to mount an all-out assault on New France. Frontenac's armies repulsed the British attack at Quebec, but in the following years French settlements in Canada were repeatedly attacked by native Iroquois forces.

Frontenac, however, continued to be more concerned with expanding the fur trade than defeating the enemy. In 1696, under strict orders

from his superiors, he led an expedition that burned down two native villages.

Frontenac died in Quebec on November 28, 1698; the war between England and France continued until 1700. It took another year before a peace treaty could be agreed between Frontenac's successor and the Iroquois. Though his governorship was controversial, Frontenac's involvement in the fur trade was very successful in expanding France's influence into the New World.

SEE ALSO

FUR TRADE ▪ IROQUOIS ▪ NEW FRANCE ▪ QUEBEC CITY

▲ *In 1690 English forces under Sir William Phips laid siege to Quebec. The English commander requested Frontenac's surrender, to which he famously replied, "My guns will give my answer." His shrewd leadership enabled Quebec to withstand the siege.*

FRONTIER

As the American colonies prospered and the population increased, people began to uproot and move westward to occupy new lands. Settlers from all the colonies moved west, drawn by the economic opportunities, and seeking freedom from religious persecution. The lure of migration was greater in the middle colonies than in New England, where people were bound by stronger ties to their towns and villages. Nevertheless in some areas it was common for as many as one person in five to leave in any given year.

BACKWOODS

In 1700 the population of the English colonies was about 350,000. Most people lived in coastal settlements and were reluctant to lose their attachment to the Old World. The frontier marked the edge of Europeanized America and was seen as a potentially hostile environment. It was not a desirable place to visit or live. The western lands were called the backcountry or backwoods. Explorations to the west, the "back of civilization," were carried out by backwoodsmen.

The frontier was also the most important point of contact between contrasting cultures: European, Native-American, and African. Relations sometimes turned violent, and many frontier settlers lived in constant fear of Native-American attack. Settlers in the frontier territories also shared ideas and folkways. In the frontier areas of New England more than 1,000 natives were converted to Christianity and granted land.

Sometimes the positions were reversed. In a few cases British

settlers captured by Native-American tribes refused to return to European settlements, preferring to stay among their captors.

In frontier areas settled by the Spanish (New Mexico, Texas, and Florida) there was a high rate of intermarriage between whites, Native Americans, and the African slaves of the Spanish. The mixed-blood children of these marriages were called mestizos. Although mestizos were accepted with little racial prejudice in the Spanish-ruled territories, only whites could move to the top of the ruling class.

FRENCH TERRITORY

France was the most successful at true cultural exchange along the frontier. In parts of present-day Canada and Michigan official French policy encouraged intermarriage between Native Americans and French settlers. Although some government officials

▲ *A traveler leads his pack horse through a pass in the Appalachian Mountains. Making the same journey in winter was considerably more difficult.*

had Native-American wives, it was the *coureurs de bois,* engaged in the fur trade along the frontier, who made it a point to live among Native Americans. Learning Native-American languages and ways, many *coureurs de bois* took Native-American wives and raised families. The children of this mixed heritage were called metis. Today the metis are a recognized culture in Canada.

The French also established forts along the frontier such as Fort Michilimackinac in 1715. Today it is called Mackinaw City, Michigan. Many families of mixed French and Native-American blood settled within the shadow of the fort. This cultural blending did not proceed as smoothly in French-owned Louisiana. Native-American and African slaves on large plantations escaped whenever the

▷ *Frontier life was often lonely. During the winter families were sometimes cut off for months by snow and flooding.*

▽ *The Appalachians formed a natural obstacle to westward expansion. The discovery of the Cumberland Gap and other mountain passes overcame the problem.*

opportunity arose, and they often ran away to live in exile along the frontier. These people, known as maroons or runaways, participated in several uprisings against the French colonial authorities.

NEW HORIZONS
By 1760 America's population approached 1.6 million. A new pioneering spirit emerged among the colonists, and they looked westward to a new frontier. Americans now saw themselves as looking forward to the west rather than backward to Europe. An observer in 1788 wrote of Americans "pushing forward" and described a stream of wagons heading west through the Appalachian Mountains. The mountains formed a kind of giant funnel, channeling settlers away from settled coastal regions into the vast unknown.

The new lands were opened by new generations of settlers from the east. Many of them made the difficult trek through the Great Valley, a route known as the Wilderness Road, which led southwestward from Pennsylvania into Kentucky. The peoples who settled these areas were from mixed backgrounds, with the French settling

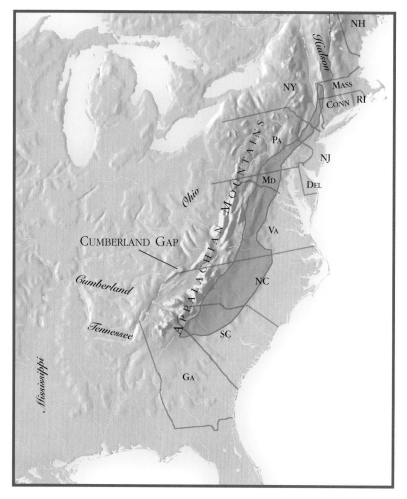

to the northeast and the Spanish in the southwest. The French and Spanish settlers' alliances with the native peoples led the British government to establish a defensive zone along the Appalachian borders. They were able to persuade various groups of settlers to move into these dangerous areas by granting them greater religious freedom.

THE FORBIDDEN LANDS

Waves of people moved into and through the Great Valley. They included Scots-Irish followers of the Presbyterian Church, French Huguenots, and English and Welsh Quakers. Their presence made a strong barrier to the fur-trading French and their native allies to the west. Georgia also became a buffer zone when English paupers, freed from debtors prison, were drawn to the colony with the promise of free land. Their presence protected the planters of South Carolina against the Spanish threat from Florida.

In the north and west Native-American and French fur traders became increasingly hostile toward the English, whom they felt were encroaching on their hunting and fur-

trapping lands. Partly as a result of this the English decided to halt further westward expansion. The Royal Proclamation of 1763 reserved all lands between the Appalachians, the Floridas, the Mississippi, and Quebec for Native Americans. Few of the colonists obeyed the order, which banned them from the newly granted native lands. Many settlers were already living beyond the Proclamation Line, and they ignored the British Crown and continued to move west.

Many settlers, angered by the proclamation and the lack of military protection, took out their frustrations on the British authorities. Pennsylvania's Paxton Boys committed atrocities against Native Americans and marched in protest on Philadelphia in 1764.

SEE ALSO

COUREURS DE BOIS ▪ FUR TRADE
▪ GEORGIA ▪ IMMIGRATION, ENGLISH ▪
IMMIGRATION, FRENCH ▪ IMMIGRATION,
SPANISH ▪ METIS AND MESTIZOS

▼ *A settler on the frontier warns of an impending Cherokee attack. One of the many uncertainties of frontier life was the threat of hostile natives.*

EYEWITNESS

IN 1774 VIRGINIA'S ROYAL GOVERNOR LORD DUNMORE SUMMED UP THE FRONTIER SPIRIT OF THE NEW WORLD AND ITS COLONISTS WHEN HE WROTE:

❝ *The established authority of any government in America, and the policy of the Government at home, are both insufficient to restrain Americans...They acquire no attachment to place: but wandering about seems engrafted in their nature; and it is a weakness incident to it, that they should forever imagine the lands further off, are still better than those upon which they are already settled.* ❞

FUNERALS

Life was difficult for the early colonial settlers. Many died during the crossing of the Atlantic, and many more fell victim to disease soon after they had landed and before they ever saw their dream of a new world fulfilled. At first there were no proper graveyards to bury the dead. Although historians are still trying to find out more about the way in which the early colonists conducted funerals, there is a general agreement that until about 1660 the rituals of burial were very simple affairs. No separate gravestones were erected above a grave, and a common plot usually served all the family. There were no sermons and no wake in which the mourners gave presents or feasted.

COMMUNITY BURIALS

It was the custom in 17th-century England to have communal burials, often without coffins. In New England the burial plot was generally close to the home of the family rather than in the grounds of the church. Puritans in particular favored this type of funeral, partly as a reaction against the elaborate Catholic funerals of Europe. It would have been difficult for them to do much else. Because there were no mortuaries and no facilities to embalm the body, the family of the deceased would look after the body until the burial day. Communities were much closer than is usually the case today, and it was common practice for the whole settlement to attend the burial.

However, as the colonists became more established, burial rituals became much more elaborate. In New England in the 1680s the English custom of giving gifts to mourners,

such as gloves and rings, became popular. How much a family gave the mourners became a way of showing how well-off it was. It was also the custom to give a gift to the minister attending the funeral. A clergyman who stayed 32 years at the North Church in Boston, for example, had no fewer than 2,940 pairs of gloves by the end of his time there.

Settlers also began to adopt the practice of erecting individual gravestones. At first, the symbols on gravestones tended to be very gloomy, but by the 1700s they were incorporating more positive, attractive designs such as cherubs.

Because there were so many different communities with different beliefs and customs, it is impossible to

▲ *Early colonial headstones were decorated with rather gruesome images of death, such as the skull and cross bones.*

▶ *The grave of John Wilkins, who died in 1710. He lies in Copp's Hill Burying Ground in Boston, which has been in use as a cemetery since 1660.*

generalize about funerals in colonial America, but the pattern of simple rites giving way from the 1660s to much more costly and organized rituals was a general trend.

In the Chesapeake Bay colonies elaborate wakes were organized, and there are records of mourners drinking and eating enormous quantities. In 1661 the cost of the funeral festivities of a man in Lower Norfolk was reckoned to be the equivalent of 2,000 lbs (907 kg) of tobacco—a huge sum of money that paid for quantities of beef, cider, and all the accompaniments. At the funeral of a planter in Charles County a year later several barrels of beer were drunk over two days, and the man, though not especially wealthy, was seen off with a volley of gunfire.

RITES AND RITUALS

Native-American tribes had elaborate funeral rites that sometimes lasted for days and involved periods of fasting, drinking, and feasting. All the tribes

▲ There were no graveyards for soldiers who died in action. The British general Edward Braddock, killed at Fort Duquesne in 1755, was buried at Great Meadows in Pennsylvania.

had their own separate rituals, some of which must have horrified the settlers. For example, following the death of a Natchez chief called Tattooed Serpent in 1725, eight of his wives, servants, and high officials were ceremonially killed.

SEE ALSO

RELIGION, NATIVE AMERICAN
RELIGION, PURITAN ■ SLAVE CULTURE

EYEWITNESS

SLAVES USUALLY MADE AN EFFORT TO BURY THEIR DEAD ACCORDING TO THEIR AFRICAN HERITAGE. THIS IS A DESCRIPTION OF A SLAVE BURYING HIS CHILD.

❝ *...its father buried with it a small bow and several arrows; a little bag of parched meal; a miniature canoe, about a foot long, and a little paddle (with which he said it would cross the ocean to his own country)...a piece of white muslin with several curious and strange figures painted on it in blue and red, by which, he said his relations would know the infant to be his son...He cut a lock of hair from his head, threw it upon the dead infant and closed the grave with his own hands.* ❞

FUR TRADE

When the first explorers from Europe arrived on the eastern seaboard of North America in the 16th century, they found a country that was teeming with wildlife. Not only could they hunt the animals for food, during the harsh winters the settlers also saw the value of the warm clothing made from the skins of animals such as beaver, mink, marten, otter, bear, and deer that was worn by Native Americans.

The explorers and the settlers began to exchange goods carried with them from Europe for the skins. Iron ax heads, cheap textiles, whiskey, and guns were traded for stacks of furs from animals trapped by the Native Americans. The trade in furs grew quickly, due mainly to a huge demand for skins in European

countries, which had almost led to the extinction in Europe of the beaver, bear, and deer populations.

A PROFITABLE BUSINESS

The most successful fur-trading enterprise, the Hudson's Bay Company, was established in England on May 2, 1670. Over the next two centuries its investors grew rich on profits from the fur trade. Beaver skins, used to make men's hats, were particularly popular, as were deer or buckskins that tailors fashioned into riding breeches and boots. East Coast settlements and ports grew prosperous on the trade in furs, which were brought from the wild interior of the country by rugged trappers who learned to trade with the Native Americans and to live their way of

▲ A white trapper, heavily laden with furs and supplies and accompanied by his pack horse, stops in a stream to water his horses. Notice the beaded belt hanging from his saddle—trappers often acquired items such as these in their exchanges with the native tribes.

life. France was more heavily engaged in the fur trade than any other nation during the colonial period. French settlements in Canada and the northern English colonies were established primarily as trading posts. A specific term was even coined, the *coureurs de bois*, for the unlicensed fur traders operating in Quebec during the 17th and 18th centuries.

A "BUCK" APIECE

So important were furs and deerskins to the economy of the early colonies that they were used as currency. It is generally believed that the term "buck"—meaning a dollar—comes from the value of a buckskin. People talked in the 18th century of selling "10 bucksworth of goods." In 1700 over 58,000 furs and skins were sent to England from Virginia alone, but despite their important contribution to the colonial economy, the fur trappers and traders were never regarded highly by the other settlers. This was largely because they lived like Native Americans, traveling the rivers by bark canoe and sleeping in the open. With the profits from their trapping expeditions they bought

cheap liquor and got drunk in the coastal settlements. Many of the settlers regarded this behavior as shameful. Benjamin Franklin described them once as "the most vicious and abandoned wretches of our nation."

Relations between the trappers and the Native Americans sometimes became hostile, too. The custom of trading guns for furs, which was opposed by many colonial leaders, provided the native tribes with a new type of weapon that enabled them to fight their enemies on more equal terms than their traditional weapons had previously allowed.

Know All Men By These Prents that Daniel Boone hath Deposited Six, vi, beaver Skins in my keep in good order and of the worth of vi shillings each skin and i Have took from them vi shillings for the keep of them and when they Be sold i will pay the balance of XXX shillings for the whole lot to any person who presents this certificate an delivers it up to Me at My keep Louisville falls of Ohio May 20 1784
John Sanders

▲ *A receipt given to the legendary American frontiersman Daniel Boone in 1784, when he was working as a trapper.*

◄ *European traders got most of their furs from Native-American trappers. In exchange they gave them goods that they could not make or get for themselves such as guns and metal tools.*

▶ *Otters were trapped in huge numbers by Native-American and colonial trappers.*

▼ *John Jacob Astor, the founder of the American Fur Company. By 1800 he had amassed over $250,000 from the fur trade.*

The fur and deerskin trade thrived well into the 18th century, but as the East Coast settlements spread steadily westward, conflicts arose between the trappers and fur traders and government officials, who wanted people to become farmers. To set up a farmstead, large areas of woodland—the natural habitat of the fur-bearing animals—had to be felled and turned to pasture. So European and native trappers found it increasingly difficult to find enough animal skins, mainly due to the huge numbers of animals that had been killed by previous generations. Those in pursuit of bear, beaver, mink, and deer were forced to venture further and further west, where they met with rival Spanish colonists heading up from the south and French trappers coming down from the north.

CONQUEST OF THE WEST

As well as the continual conflict with settled farmers, fur traders were forced to compete for funds with the West Indian trade in sugar and slaves, which was seen as more profitable by European investors. By the time of the Revolutionary War the fur trade had lost its former importance on the East Coast, though it remained a powerful attraction for traders in Canada and the West well into the 19th century. By that time intrepid trappers and explorers had crossed the Great Plains and were blazing trails through the Rockies and into the Arctic, continuing the pioneering tradition that opened up much of North America.

CLASH OF CULTURES

Contact with European traders often had a negative impact on native culture. Many tribal nations found it more profitable to trade with the whites than to pursue old trading links with neighboring tribes, and individuals sought personal wealth and prestige at the expense of their community. Some of the farming tribes stopped planting, and their fields became overrun with weeds. Finally, furs were often exchanged for items such as guns and alcohol that were new to native culture and were to change it forever.

SEE ALSO

BOONE, DANIEL ■ COUREURS DE BOIS ■ HUDSON'S BAY COMPANY ■ NEW FRANCE ■ QUEBEC CITY

FURNITURE

The first Jamestown settlers in 1607 remarked on the "goodly tall Trees" in the New World. Soon such immense trees were turned into boards that were used to construct ships, houses, carts, wagons, and the pieces of furniture needed for daily life. Furniture makers of all backgrounds came to the colonies throughout the 17th and 18th centuries. In the early period of colonial American history most established European craftsmen were not willing to move to America. Many of the colonial furniture makers therefore were not highly skilled and often made only simple pieces. The village craftsmen provided people with chairs, chests, settles (wooden couches that could be opened up to become beds), benches, stools, and tables. In the 18th century they added free-standing cupboards for clothes, household linens, and clothing, as well as writing desks and chests of drawers. One other item that all furniture craftsmen made was the coffin, and many of them built up a thriving side business as morticians. Tombstones were sometimes made of carved wood, and these too were produced locally.

Woodworkers known as joiners produced the panelled walls, door and window frames, mantelpieces, and staircases in houses as well as

▼ *A museum reconstruction of a 17th-century colonial "keeping room." Notice the baby's high chair (left), the highly decorated sideboards, and the wide floorboards.*

F

plain furniture. By using a lathe, wood turners could make furniture with rounded legs and rungs for ladders.

Cabinetmakers were the most skilled woodworkers. They worked with intricately curved surfaces and complex joints and had often learned the skills of turning and joining as well. Some were even skilled upholsterers, adding cloth or leather seats to their pieces of furniture. The first known cabinetmaker in the colonies was Phineas Pratt, who by 1622 was operating a shop in Plymouth Colony.

IMPORTED STYLES
During the 17th century most furniture was imported. Writing desks were the most commonly imported pieces of furniture, while large four-poster beds with massive headboards and footboards were more often made in the colonies because their size made them expensive to transport. Even in the 18th century, when homes could be furnished almost entirely with American-made furniture, the styling remained European.

The Windsor chair is a good example of how European styles of furniture were adopted by colonial society. This chair style, recognizable by slender, upright spokes in the back and hollowed-out seats for comfort, came from Britain in the 1730s. Never designed as an elegant piece, the Windsor was made from two or three types of wood and painted in various colors to match the other furnishings in a room. Although it enjoyed some popularity in British households, its

▲ *A late 17th-century oak and pine carved chest, which was made in Hampshire County, Massachusetts.*

success lasted far longer in America. Until the 1820s it was the common everyday seat in the American tavern, cottage, and farmhouse. Every village cabinetmaker turned them out, and some city craftsmen made nothing but Windsors. In Philadelphia, which became the center of Windsor chair production, the chair makers received orders from all over the country.

COLONIAL STYLE
All of the colonial regions developed recognizable furniture styles by the 18th century. In the larger New England towns, such as Boston and Salem, skilled craftsmen produced both elaborate and more conservatively styled pieces that were influenced by European tastes. New York continued to reflect the influence of its early Dutch settlers.

▶ *A blue-painted Windsor chair made in New England during the late 18th century. Years of use have worn the paint from the chair arms.*

▲ An expensively furnished late 18th-century drawing room in Salem, Massachusetts.

Pennsylvania, particularly around Philadelphia, was strongly German in its fashion. Virginia, and to a lesser extent the Carolinas, reflected the most popular British fashions.

Because of their close ties to Britain, a distinctive style did not develop in these areas until late in the 18th century. In fact, residents who could afford it still ordered most of their furniture from Britain rather than rely on what they considered crude "country-made" pieces. In Virginia cabinetmakers of note operated in Williamsburg. The first to appear in the records was a man called Peter Scott who operated there from 1732 until the 1770s.

Although furniture making was slow to develop in most of the colonies, by the time of the Revolutionary War cabinetmakers no longer relied on Europe for skilled labor or supplies. American native woods like black walnut, black cherry, or maple were used. Finer pieces were fashioned by colonial craftsmen from cedar and mahogany shipped from the Caribbean, and these helped to create a distinctively American style of furniture.

SEE ALSO

FORESTRY ■ IMMIGRATION, ENGLISH ■ IMMIGRATION, GERMAN

▼ This lounger, or "day bed," was made in early 18th-century Philadelphia and is fashioned in the "William and Mary" style— named for the English monarchs during whose reign the style became popular.

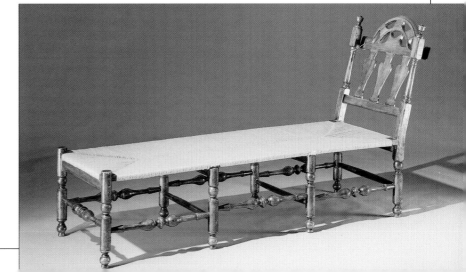

GAMES AND SPORTS

The Puritans brought a rich heritage of sports and games with them from England. Their kings were sportsmen: Henry VIII enjoyed his falconry and horseback riding in Tudor times, and his daughter Elizabeth I took after him, rejoicing in her gaming expeditions to Epping Forest, where she stayed at her hunting lodge and went shooting. She also enjoyed festive occasions when archery, stickball games, and fencing matches were held.

Some of the sports popular in England at the time were bloody and cruel; "gander-pulling" involved pulling the heads of geese in tug-of-war-like games; cock-fighting, where two roosters fought each other, was also popular. These sports continued to entertain the colonial settlers.

However, it was illegal to take part in any game on the Sabbath day—Sunday—since it had to be reserved for religious worship.

GAMES FOR OLD AND YOUNG

Adults in English settlements played tennis, badminton, croquet, cricket, rounders (similar to baseball but played with a larger, softer ball), quoits (like the game of horseshoes), and a form of football similar to modern-day soccer.

Children had vast, unpopulated fields and woods to play in and were able to take advantage of these open spaces on Saturdays and weekdays. They had few toys, however, and those they did have were simple and often home-made. They rolled hoops, played marbles, jumped over each

▲ *George Washington, like most of his fellow army officers, was a skilled horseman and regularly took part in foxhunts.*

▶ *This notice was printed in* Rivington's Gazette, *which was published in New York, on October 17, 1776. Horse-racing was made popular in the area by the Dutch settlers.*

G

The men of the community play a game of bowls outside a tavern, which is keeping the players supplied with tankards of ale.

other in games of leapfrog, flew kites, and played hopscotch and tipcat (batting a wooden spindle back and forth). Colonial elders would often cast a disapproving eye on even these simple amusements, since they were not seen as ways to "increase the glory of God." However, church leaders did agree that "small amusements and sporting games on weekdays" were acceptable as long as they were "restrained."

If settler families felt slightly hemmed-in by these restrictions, they could pick up their rods and go fishing. Fishing escaped religious disapproval perhaps because it provided food for the table—and it became the most popular sport of the 17th century for men and boys. Even Cotton Mather, one of the strictest colonial preachers, found fishing acceptable; he often used fishing tales when preaching to his children.

Fishing was an English sport that the New Englanders had inherited, and they discovered a new-found freedom in this recreation. An early Massachusetts law guaranteed every resident "free fishing and fowling." The only restriction was imposed at the end of the 17th century to prevent fishing during the spawning season when fish lay their eggs—a sensible precaution against overfishing.

The children of Maine and Massachusetts particularly liked mackerel fishing. There are great shoals of these tasty, silvery fish around the jagged shores of New England, and they are easy to catch and delicious to eat. Even young children brought home impressive catches for the dinner table.

WINTER PASTIMES
Winter sports were understandably more popular in the northern colonies. Adolescent New Englanders had the advantage of long, cold winters that created the freezing conditions ideal for games such as tobogganing, sleighing, and skating. The Puritans viewed sports that contributed to travel as partly "useful toil," so they imposed few restrictions. In the French colonies in Quebec the settlers were discovering the pleasures of ice-skating, and they also developed a game that involved batting a wooden puck between the

LONG-ISLAND HORSE RACE.
To be run for, on Thurſday the 6th of November next, at the New Lots, on Long-Iſland, about ſeven miles from Brooklyn ferry, a PURSE, value ONE HUNDRED DOLLARS, or upwards, by three years old colts or fillies, the beſt of three heats, one mile to each heat; three quarter blood carrying eight ſtone, half blood ſeven ſtone nine pounds, &c. &c. ------All horſes running for the above purſe to pay one guinea entrance; which money will be run for the next day by all except the winning horſe the firſt day.

PUBLIC AUCTION.
On Monday morning, 11 o'clock, at the coffee-houſe, will be ſold, a fine large black horſe, only 5 years old, fit either for ſaddle or chair.
On Tueſday, a quantity of Barcelona wine in

G players with crude sticks—the forerunner of the exhilarating modern game of ice hockey.

The southern colonies tended to cling to their English heritage even more enthusiastically than their northern counterparts. The leading leisure pastimes in colonies such as Virginia, the Carolinas, and Maryland—fox-hunting, cock-fighting, horseback riding, racing, golfing, boating, and dancing—had a distinctly English character. Dancing was a popular pastime among all classes. On the large plantations of the South grand balls were a part of the social

▶ *A Puritan governor interrupts the Christmas sports outside a tavern and delivers a stern lecture to the revellers.*

▼ *The champion ball player of the Choctaw tribe. The native ball-game was very similar to lacrosse.*

scene, while even the poorest settlers could enjoy an evening's dancing with their family and friends. Many of the favorite dances were traditional ones brought from the settlers' homelands, such as Scottish Highland dancing.

RACING TIMES
In the latter part of the 17th century Virginia landowners imported 176 thoroughbred horses from England and started their own horsebreeding stables. Dutch settlers had a similar fondness for horse racing, and freedom from the strict controls of the English Puritans, who preached passionately on the evils of gambling, enabled them to hold regular horse races in the New Netherland colonies. The Dutch established permanent track racing in upstate New York; the bustling town of Saratoga developed into the horse-racing center of the New World until the English occupied New Netherland in 1664.

One of the most popular Dutch games was "curling," in which the players used curved sticks to hit balls across the ground or ice; there are elements of the game in the modern sports of bowls, golf, ice hockey, and field hockey.

EYEWITNESS

CAPTAIN JOHN SMITH, ONE OF THE EARLY COLONISTS AT JAMESTOWN, WAS AN AVID FISHERMAN AND ENCOURAGED HIS FELLOW SETTLERS TO TAKE UP THE SPORT.

66 *What pleasure can there be more than to recreate themselves before their own doores in their own Boats upon the sea where man, woman and childe, with a small hooke and line, by angling, may take divers sorts of excellent Fish at their pleasures...* 99

Inns and taverns in New England were notorious havens for gambling and drinking. Both were seen as deeply sinful acts, and so they tended to take place away from home, hearth, and churchmen. Men drank hard and played hard, throwing bowls, hitting skittles, hurling darts at dart boards, and playing for high stakes at poker. Respectable women did not go near the taverns.

Pious New Englanders became more and more critical of horse racing until, in 1677, they banned it altogether. In general, they tended to frown on spectator sports—which they referred to as "contrived" sports—and favored "natural" sports that everyone could play. This did not mean they did not enjoy tough sports, however—wrestling, boxing, and fencing flourished.

While many would like to claim that baseball was invented in America, it may be a descendant of the British game rounders. Rounders was played regularly in the colonies. A player hits the ball with a bat and runs around the bases in a counterclockwise direction. It did not become the leaner, meaner game we know today with the smaller, hard ball until the

1850s when Mark Twain drew a comparison between baseball and the young American nation, saying that the game characterized the "drive and push" of the country.

SEE ALSO
CHEROKEE ■ FISHING ■ FOOD AND DRINK ■ HUNTING ■ NEW NETHERLAND

▼ *Men betting on a fight in a "cockpit." The fight between the two specially bred roosters only ended when one had been killed.*

FURTHER READING

Anderson, Joan. **A Williamsburg Household**. *New York: Clarion Books, 1988.*

Barrett, Tracy. **Growing up in Colonial America**. *Brookfield, Connecticut: The Milbrook Press, 1995.*

Bosco, Peter L. **Roanoke: The Lost Colony**. *Brookfield, Connecticut: The Milbrook Press, 1992.*

Bowen, Gary. **Stranded at Plimoth Plantation 1629**. *New York: HarperCollins Publishers, 1994.*

Carter, Alden R. **The Colonial Wars**. *New York: Franklin Watts, 1992.*

Clare, John D., ed. **The Voyages of Christopher Columbus**. *San Diego: Gulliver Books (HBJ), 1992.*

Daugherty, James. **The Landing of the Pilgrims**. *New York: Random House, 1978.*

Erdosh, George. **Food & Recipes of the 13 Colonies**. *New York: PowerKids Press, 1997.*

Fritz, Jean. **The Double Life of Pocahontas**. *New York: Puffin Books, 1983.*

Hakim, Joy. **The First Americans**. *New York: Oxford University Press, 1993.*

Hakim, Joy. **Making Thirteen Colonies**. *New York: Oxford University Press, 1993.*

Hakim, Joy. **From Colonies to Country**. *New York: Oxford University Press, 1993.*

Kalman, Bobbie. **Colonial Life**. *New York: Crabtree Publishing, 1992.*

Kalman, Bobbie. **Historic Communities: A Colonial Town—Williamsburg**. *New York: Crabtree Publishing, 1992.*

Kent, Deborah. **African Americans in the Thirteen Colonies**. *New York: Childrens Press, 1988.*

Lenski, Lois. **Indian Captive: The Story of Mary Jemison**. *New York: HarperTrophy, 1969.*

Roach, Marilynne K. **In the Days of the Salem Witchcraft Trials**. *Boston: Houghton Mifflin Co., 1996.*

Roop, Connie and Peter, eds. **Pilgrim Voices: Our First Year in the New World**. *New York: Walkers and Company, 1995.*

Tunis, Edwin. **Shaw's Fortune: The Picture Story of a Colonial Plantation**. *Cleveland: The World Publishing Company, 1966.*

Speare, Elizabeth George. **The Witch of Blackbird Pond**. *Boston: Houghton Mifflin Co., 1958.*

Washburne, Carolyn Kott. **A Multicultural Portrait of Colonial Life**. *New York: Marshall Cavendish, 1994.*

Waters, Kate. **Tapenum's Day: A Wampanoag Indian Boy in Pilgrim Times**. *New York: Scholastic Press, 1996.*

Yenne, Bill, ed. **Our Colonial Period: The Chronicle of American History from 1607 to 1770**. *San Francisco: Bluewood Books, 1996.*

SET INDEX

Volume numbers and main entries are shown in **bold**. Page numbers of illustrations or captions are shown in *italic* or ***bold italic*** if they are in main articles.

The editors wish to thank Peter Wallenstein, Associate
Professor of History at Virginia Polytechnic Institute and
State University, for his help in preparing this volume.

Picture Credits
AKG London 164, 189 Biblioteca del Palacio Real, Madrid 166t
The American Museum in Britain, Bath 199, 225
Biofotos/G.Kinns 175b The Bridgeman Art Library 204t, 208t
The British Museum 188 Carnegie Institute, Pittsburg 184-5
Kennedy Galleries 178t Philip Mould Historical Portraits 210
Reynolds Museum, Winston, Salem, N.Carolina 174-5, 218-9 Royal
Albert Memorial Museum, Exeter 176 Stapleton Collection 177
State Historical Society of Wisconsin 214b Christie's Images 226,
227b Corbis 170b William Bake 186 A. Griffiths Belt 203 Bettmann
172t, 191, 194t, 222 Library of Congress cover, 169, 197, 221t

Roy Corral 224t Edifice 221b Dave G.Houser 173t Hulton 231 Joe
McDonald 174b North Carolina Museum of Art 180b Philadelphia
Museum 180t, 209 E.Rotkin 213 R.Hamilton Smith 184b
Ecoscene/Chinch Gryniewicz 165t, 206 Paul Thompson 202b
ET Archive/New York Public Library 182, 196, 196-7, 198 Mary
Evans Picture Library 171b, 181b, 192b, 195, 201tr, 211, 215t,
216, 223b Werner Forman Archive/National Museum of
Denmark 166b Angelo Hornak Library 200t, 227t Hulton
Getty 172-3, 204b, 205 Peter Newark's American Pictures front
cover , title page, 165b, 167, 168c, 168t, 171t, 178b, 179, 183, 185b,
187, 190, 192t, 193b, 194b, 200b, 202t, 207, 208b, 212, 214t, 215b,
217, 219b, 220, 223t, 224cl, 228, 229b, 229t, 230b, 230-1

Maps by John Woolford: 195, 213, 218